GILERA
ROAD RACERS

OSPREY
COLLECTOR'S
LIBRARY

GILERA
ROAD RACERS

From Milan to the Mountain

Raymond Ainscoe

Published in 1987 by Osprey Publishing Limited
27A Floral Street, London WC2E 9DP
Member company of the George Philip Group

British Library Cataloguing in Publication Data

Ainscoe, Raymond
    Gilera road racers.——(Osprey collector's
    library)
    1. Gilera motorcycle——History
    I. Title
    629.2'275   TL448.G5
ISBN 0–85045–675–4

Editor Tony Thacker
Design Paul Butters

Filmset by Tameside Filmsetting Limited,
Ashton-under-Lyne, Lancashire
Printed by BAS Printers Limited,
Over Wallop, Hampshire

Contents

Foreword by
Phil Read MBE

The Golden Jubilee of the famous TT races in the Isle of Man in 1957 welcomed the cream of the world's racing motorcycles, raced by riders who were and would become household names: Surtees, McIntyre, Dale, Hartle and Brett.

I watched this, my first TT, at the bottom of Barregarrow, a fast downhill left-hand bend with a high granite wall on the inside and trees on the outside. Within a few minutes of the start of the eight-lap Senior we heard the wail, scream and rumble of the approaching machines. The MV Agusta of Surtees flashed into view, looking almost out of control as it missed the outside kerb by inches. As Surtees turned on the power the spectators around me jumped backwards off the bank or behind the trees.

The Nortons rushed through as if on rails but down on power. Campbell's single-cylinder Moto Guzzi was deceptively fast and steady. The V8 Moto Guzzi looked most powerful, but Dale seemed unsure how to use it, wishing he were on the smooth and fast Monza track.

The Gileras of Bob McIntyre and Bob Brown arrived; Mac looked so aggressively fast that he took my breath away. On this most difficult, demanding and longest race circuit in the world, the two Gileras looked winners all the way. We all stood and cheered when Bob Mac broke the 100 mph lap on his first flyer.

Until their strange decision to pull out at the end of the 1957 season, in their last years of GP racing the 500 cc Gilera had set the ultimate standard, sought after by other makes. Such was the aura created by Gilera together with Geoff Duke that whenever the maestro wheeled this machine on to the start line, the crowds would rise in wonder and respect for the near perfect combination of man and machine.

Phil Read MBE
125 cc World Champion 1968
250 cc World Champion 1964, 1965, 1968, 1971
500 cc World Champion 1973, 1974
F1 World Champion 1977

Chobham, Surrey
4 September 1986

Phil Read riding to Gold Cup success on the Scuderia Duke 500 cc Gilera at Scarborough in 1963

Acknowledgements

In a four-year search for information for this book, I count myself fortunate to have met innumerable riders, mechanics, journalists and enthusiasts, all of whom have been enthralled by the Gilera fable. I have been overwhelmed by their collective assistance for which I express my gratitude.

I am particularly grateful to Piero Taruffi, Dorino Serafini, Massimo Masserini, the Milani brothers, Denis Jenkinson, Luigi Colombo and Derek Minter, all of whom scoured their memories for tales of distant seasons. To Franco Passoni, still an inhabitant of Arcore, goes my appreciation for his recollections of the design work during the Golden Age of the 1950s. To Paolo Gornati, a long-serving Gilera stalwart, to Fernando Bruscoli of, dare I say it, the Benelli club of Pesaro, and to Roberto Patrignani, I owe a special acknowledgement of indebtedness for their unstinted hospitality as I toured Italy seeking interviews and photographs.

For their assistance with the provision of photographs to illustrate the text, I must record my thanks to the following: Dr Helmut Krackowizer, Mick Woollett, Nick Nicholls, Louis Pauzin, *Moto Revue*, S.R. Keig Limited, Brian Woolley and EMAP.

I should also thank Tim Parker, the former editor of Osprey, for his encouragement and guidance as the idea of the project germinated, and Phil Read, not only for his recollections of a season aboard a 'camel', but also for kindly agreeing to write the Foreword. Finally, to Signora Gigliola Carnielli Gilera goes my gratitude for her hospitality and the provision of photographs from her family album.

Raymond Ainscoe
10 September 1986

1 | The early years: 1909–35

The first Gilera—a pushrod 317 cc machine from 1909

In the pioneer days of motorcycle sport in Italy, the Como–Brunate hillclimb was an established fixture in the calendar. The switchback three-mile track ran from the provincial capital of Como, at the southern tip of the lake of that name, to its hill-hugging suburb of Brunate, nestling over 1500 ft above the waters. Even in its heyday the competition hardly ranked as a classic, but two meetings merit recall. The 1908 edition was won in record time by a young

·1909·

mechanic who was on the brink of a career which would bring him some repute as a rider but much greater renown as a constructor. The novice repeated his success in 1909 with one significant difference—the Bucher which had carried him to victory a year earlier had been discarded and his mount now bore his own name, Gilera.

Giuseppe Gilera was born on 21 December 1887, at Zelobuonpersico, a hamlet to the south-east of Milan, into a farming family of distinctly modest means. At the age of 15, armed with little in the way of a formal education, Giuseppe began an apprenticeship with the motorcycle firm established by the Milanese bicycle manufacturer Edoardo Bianchi. He soon passed on to refine his skills as a mechanic with the Italian branch of the Swiss Moto Reve company, including a spell in Geneva, and subsequently thence to the long-since-forgotten Bucher concern, by which time he was participating in the burgeoning sport. But the youthful Gilera was more than an assiduous mechanic and an aspiring competitor; he was also an incipient businessman, and in 1909, in a tiny workshop in Milan, he built a motorcycle to his own design.

It must be admitted that the first Gilera bore an uncanny resemblance to the contemporary Bucher. Its frame was, in keeping with the times, a bicycle type, duly beefed up, with front forks which were generally unsprung, although some later models were graced with a pair of vertical side springs, while the only brake was fitted to the rear wheel, acting on the internal circumference of the belt rim. The pedal-assisted, single-cylinder engine was a little less conventional, being of pushrod design. Measuring 67×90 mm for a capacity of 317 cc, with a heavily finned cast-iron head and barrel, it produced a healthy 7 bhp at 3000 rpm, which was sufficient to propel the

Giuseppe Gilera aboard one of his first side-valve models

165 lb machine to a purported top speed of over 60 mph. Other features were the usual belt drive, a front-mounted chain-driven magneto, a short stub exhaust, a Binks carburettor, and a $1\frac{1}{2}$-gallon petrol tank on which 'G. Gilera' was obtrusively emblazoned.

The sport in Italy was taking root in the years before the Great War, particularly with the foundation in 1911 of the Moto Club d'Italia as a governing body for the heretofore heterogeneous local clubs. To celebrate the auspicious occasion, the national daily sports paper *La Gazzetta dello Sport* organized a Festival of Speed at the Trotter track in Milan, inviting all the leading riders of the day. The meeting saw the début of a Gilera team, to give a grandiose title to an *ad hoc* assembly, for Pisani and Sassi, two of the local regulars, had been invited to ride the unsprung 317 cc machines. It was left to the young entrepreneur to collect the squad's laurels by winning a heat, although he was beaten in the final by the other heat winner, the Torinese Clemente Merlo (SIAMT), who was later to become a Gilera agent. In these early years, Gilera readily entered his machines in any type of competition: long-distance epics, hillclimbs, on the boards or local road races, such as that on the Cremona circuit, where he obtained his most notable pre-war success with a class victory in 1912 when he covered the 120 miles at over 40 mph.

A major breakthrough came when he struck up an acquaintance with a lawyer, the proud but frustrated possessor of a fickle Harley-Davidson which had thus far resisted all attempts to coax it into reliability. When Gilera's touch did the trick, the lawyer recommended the talented mechanic to his well-heeled friends. Gilera soon ventured into manufacture of side-valve models, a single being followed by a twin. Gradual expansion necessitated moving premises, initially across the street in Milan from number 42 to 39 on Corso XXII Marzo and subsequently out to Arcore, a prosperous village just beyond the industrial city

Giuseppe Gilera at the Trotter track in Milan

of Monza. Alas, Gilera's consolidation was interrupted by the First World War, during which bicycles were turned out for the army, but by 1920 he was back in motorcycle production.

Gilera was beset by another calamity during these turbulent years. Riding at night on country roads, he was struck by an unlit lorry. His severe injuries included the loss of a lung and compelled him to remain in hospital for many months. Although he was never again to ride competitively at the highest level, he recovered full health and remained an active sportsman until the end of his days, being particularly enamoured of yachting and hunting.

Two of Gilera's characteristics, both of which were to exercise a profound influence on the factory's racing involvement during the years to come, were already apparent. Firstly, in the Italian manner, he placed considerable reliance on his family's skills and devotion. His younger brother Luigi, although not of a businesslike frame of mind, was soon at his side as mechanic, rider and factotum. Gilera had married a local girl, Ida Grana, and her three brothers were to run substantial Gilera agencies. Indeed, one of them, Rosolino, was the most consistently successful rider of the sports models during the 1920s. Another brother-in-law, Pierino Bernasconi, who had married one of the Grana sisters,

was an accountant and was subsequently brought in to oversee the bureaucratic side of the company. As the years passed, a Gilera village grew around the family's villa, which was virtually in the factory yard, and long-standing employees and their dependants were willingly brought within the Gilera fold. Gilera's generosity extended to granting interest-free loans and cash gifts to members of his workforce to enable them to buy properties in Arcore. The methods of the self-made industrialist of humble origins were far removed from the high-handed despotism associated with the aristocratic Count Agusta of MV fame; rather he engendered a family

One of the pre-war models with Giuseppe Gilera on the far left

The first squad, assembled at the Trotter track in 1911, featuring Sassi, Pisani and Gilera

atmosphere among his employees, as he would later with his riders, earning himself a clan-like loyalty and respect which lingers still in Arcore, more than 15 years after his death.

Secondly, Giuseppe Gilera, although undoubtedly a keen sportsman, was principally a businessman, concerned to develop his flourishing enterprise without rocking its sound economic basis. Indeed, expansion continued apace, prompting a further and final move in 1925 to a larger site on the outskirts of Arcore which is occupied today by the Gilera section of the Piaggio empire. Accordingly, throughout the 1920s and early 1930s, financial prudence

dictated that the company's inherent sporting instincts were held at arm's length by its founder. Any racing activity in these years was merely an adjunct to the business, a hobby for the proprietors. A string of bikes, generally based on production models, did represent the Arcore concern with some success in Italian road races, but to regard them as works racers is to accord them an undue eminence. As was the case with the majority of their competitors, Gilera's early and largely unsung efforts at racing must be viewed as those of enthusiastic amateurs and no more than that.

Giuseppe Gilera was, however, alert to the possibilities of promoting sales by competing with machines based on those available to the public, and so when the factory returned to racing in 1920 it was with a 500 cc bike barely changed from the production model. The simple tubular diamond-pattern frame held a side-valve engine (84 × 90 mm: 498 cc) which, initially, was good for 10 bhp at 3800 rpm. A Bosch or Marelli magneto, a three-speed hand-change gearbox, primary and final chain drive and rear wheel braking were standard. The adjustments to the so-called racing versions were few indeed. The girder forks acquired two side springs instead of the usual central vertical spring, the final drive chain was deprived of its cover as a meagre concession to weight-saving, and the petrol and oil caps were moved from the right- to the left-hand side of the black tank, which now boasted a neat emblem as well as the constructor's name.

The sports version of the side-valve model was ridden with some gusto by Luigi Gilera and the Paduan rider Gino Zanchetta, who took the marque's first post-war victory winning 'il Premio del Re' at the Circuito delle Prealpi Venete in July 1920, albeit at the relatively modest speed of 52.6 mph. Probably the most notable result attained with the machine was that of Ferdinando Martinengo, when he collected third place in the 750 cc category of the inaugural circuit of Lario in 1921. This race, held over a scenic 22-mile course by Lake Como (alias Lake Lario), was intended to be the Italian answer to the TT and for the next two decades was one of Italy's premier international races.

Racing in the peninsula received a further welcome fillip with the construction of the purpose-built Monza track, which, fortunately for Gilera, was just a couple of miles from their factory. The first GP of the Nations was held at the circuit in 1922. Gilera made a token gesture for the event by tinkering with the side-valve engine, the dimensions of which were rumoured to have been modified to 85 × 88 mm. Although Luigi Gilera nudged 80 mph and lapped at 68 mph, the machine, along with many other half-litre models, was outclassed by Ernesto Gnesa's victorious two-stroke 350 cc Garelli and soon retired from the fray.

In 1924 Gilera produced what may be fairly described as their first genuine racer, in that it was intended purely for the track and bikes were not generally available to the public. The 500 cc VT (*valvole in testa*) model was no trendsetter, although a pushrod engine had been designed with dimensions of 79 × 100 mm, capable of 18 bhp at 5000 rpm, producing a top speed approaching 100 mph. The machine borrowed most of the cycle parts from its side-valve predecessors. A novelty was the drum brake fitted to the front wheel. The three-speed gearbox was retained and the gear-driven Bosch magneto remained front-mounted.

The ohv bike's career began auspiciously in September 1924 in the long-distance Raid Nord–Sud, when Zanchetta covered the 544 miles from Milan to Naples at 30.11 mph to win the 500 cc class. Although the machine's reliability was proven, its speed patently left something to be desired, as overall victory fell to Edoardo Self's Bianchi of a meagre 350 cc.

The pushrod machine was the mainstay of the factory's racing effort for the next ten years, during which period the only major redesign occurred in 1929 with the acquisition of a saddle tank and a revised frame. In the lesser events the VT racer was respectably competitive, earning sporadic victories. For example, Luigi Gilera's success at Crema in 1925 at 55.75 mph was repeated by Giusto Zaro in 1926 and 1928 at 59.65 mph and 68.35 mph respectively. Giuseppe Gilera chipped in with victory in the veterans' class on his old stamping ground at the Como–Brunate hillclimb in 1930.

In the more prestigious events, the bike's performances were markedly lack-lustre, coming nearest to a classic victory in 1928 when Zaro was runner-up in the 500 cc category over the Lario circuit behind Mario Colombo's Sunbeam. Later that year, Grana managed third place in the GP at Monza, but it must be admitted that he finished over 12 minutes behind winner Franconi's Sunbeam in the three-hour race. The final flourish of the VT model came in 1932 with the introduction of a three-valve version, which earned a second place in the hands of Ettore Villa in the 1933 Milano–Napoli marathon in the wake of a GP Bianchi.

The racing squad, still led by Giuseppe Gilera, who attended to much of the design work and testing in his spare time, made a half-baked attempt to compete with technically more sophisticated rivals in 1927 when a single-overhead-camshaft engine was designed for the Italian GP. The cycle parts were cribbed from the ohv racer, like which it sported an oil tank between the gearbox and the rear axle. The sohc assembly was governed by a chain on the right-hand side of the engine, running behind a massive light-alloy cover, while engine dimensions reverted to those of the sv job at 84 × 90 mm. The engine produced an estimated 23 bhp at 6000 rpm, but the bike's performance must have been disappointing. Although three machines were readied for practice, they were withdrawn from the big race and never appeared again. In fact, the sohc model was, like the ohv bike before it, at least one step behind the leading contemporary designs. For example, by 1927, Tazio Nuvolari's legendary 350 cc Bianchi had been winning consistently at international level for two seasons, enjoying the boon of double overhead-camshafts, being the first racing motorcycle to be so provided.

Perversely, it was the humble sv bike which, having evolved over the years, thrust the squad into the forefront of international competition in 1930, when the Gilera team won the International Trophy at that year's ISDT based around Grenoble. Two 500 cc solos were ridden by the experienced Miro Maffeis, a former Bianchi works rider, and Rosolino Grana, while the team was completed by Luigi Gilera at the controls of the sidecar with the faithful Zanchetta nominally in the chair, although he often rode pillion. The same team, with Umberto Meani replacing Zanchetta as passenger, retained the Trophy and

won gold medals in the following year's competition held in Italy. Their opponents were favourably impressed not only by the surprising turn of speed of the sv models but also by a sporting gesture at the Monza speed trials on the last day of the 1931 event: when a New Imperial suffered the seemingly terminal disaster of a collapsed wheel, the offending item was rushed to the factory at Arcore and repaired in double-quick time free of charge.

Giuseppe Gilera, as manager of the team, established an enviable reputation for his meticulous attention to detail, personally testing all his bikes, including those of the privateers, before the competition began. He was now on the fringes of international celebrity, with sporting success based on and complemented by industrial progress. The larger premises in Arcore permitted the introduction of sophisticated production lines and, by 1931, 190 employees were turning out a dozen motorcycles every day. Interviewed for *Motor Cycling* after the second ISDT victory, Giuseppe Gilera reported that he did not intend his company to expand further, as the existing set-up was sufficiently profitable and he did not wish to endanger the congenial atmosphere that prevailed. Furthermore, he confided that, although participation in trials events would continue, there would be no official appearances on the racetracks. Within a few years, however, he was to be proved wrong.

Two factors may account for the change of heart which would see a genuine Gilera racer in the GP arena in 1937. The first was blatantly political: the prevailing regime regarded motor sport, on both two wheels and four, as a symbol of a nation's vigour; success brought in its wake the much needed coinage of status and respectability, implying, however erroneously, power and prosperity. Additionally, Mussolini was an ardent motorcycle enthusiast, being the proud possessor of membership card number one in the Italian motorcycle club, while his like-

The victorious 1931 ISDT team consisting of Miro Maffeis, Rosolino Grana, Umberto Meani and Luigi Gilera

minded sons acted as stewards at the Lario classic. Accordingly, Italian factories were given every incentive by the government to compete in international events in order to uphold the homeland's honour. The excesses of the chauvinistic regime, and perhaps more pertinently its downright incompetence, were not yet apparent and most sportsmen of the era, predominantly decent souls such as Nuvolari, toed the party line. Giuseppe Gilera was no exception and would, on occasion, don the infamous black shirt and mingle with the bemedalled Fascist hierarchy.

Nothing sinister should be read into this; it was merely standard behaviour for an industrialist whose factory was reputedly in receipt of

handsome subsidies to prepare for the ISDT. In fact, the effort was, despite press speculation to the contrary, exclusively private. One of Giuseppe's two daughters, Gigliola, was fluent in several European languages and accompanied the team on its ventures as translator; today, she remembers those early successes with crystal clarity and steadfastly denies that her father received as much as a lira from the government for his enterprise.

For whatever reason, Gilera's mind had turned to the prospect of road racing by 1933, when a

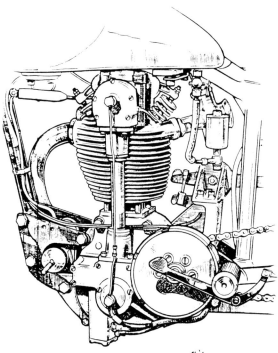

Une 500 experimentale *Gilera*
à arbre à cames en tête
(1933-34).

bevel-gear-driven sohc 500 cc single-cylinder engine was designed. Two years later, another 500 cc engine was proposed; the sohc assembly was to be driven by a gear train running up the right-hand side of the single cylinder. Both designs were, however, unceremoniously discarded without coming to fruition.

The second and crucial factor which prompted Gilera to place his machines on the Grand Prix starting grids was the offer of a ready-made, off-the-shelf winner that fell into his lap at the end of 1935.

2 | OPRA and CNA

The foundations of Gilera's impending successes had been laid in Rome in 1923. To appreciate this seemingly eccentric statement, a digression in the tale is not only justified but demanded.

Racing in the 1920s was the preserve of single-cylinder engines, such as the horizontally-mounted four-valve 500 cc Guzzi that carried Guido Mentasti to the first-ever European championship at Monza in 1924. True, the twin-cylinder engines had lingered on into the early years of the decade, with both Indian and Harley-Davidson winning Italian titles, but they were soon to be discarded as too cumbersome. As for the in-line four-cylinder engine, the most notable example of which was the Belgian FN, that was bedevilled by cooling problems for its rear cylinders and drive complications that rendered it unsuitable for racing. For all that, the day of the multi was breaking.

In 1923, two engineers, Carlo Gianini and Piero Remor, newly graduated from Rome University, installed themselves in a small workshop in the centre of the Eternal City, near the Baths of Diocletian, intent on producing a high-performance motorcycle engine. The novel feature of their proposal was that the engine's four cylinders were to be set across the frame, thereby alleviating the cooling and drive difficulties that had so beset its in-line prede-cessors. Little has been written about the first transverse four-cylinder engine that was to spawn a host of successful imitators; that which has appeared in print has undoubtedly been plagued by memory fade and riddled with yawning gaps, ambiguities and inaccuracies. It is perhaps unrealistic to expect the full story to emerge at a distance of over 60 years.

The impecunious young engineers fortuitously came to the attention of a wealthy industrialist, Count Bonmartini, who was a pioneering civil aviator by trade and an accomplished amateur car racer by inclination. In 1924 the enthusiastic noble formed a company called, democratically if a little unimaginatively, GRB (Gianini, Remor, Bonmartini), to give reality to his friends' dreams.

The team's first effort employed a single ohc assembly which was governed by bevel gears and a shaft in front of and between the four vertical cylinders, which were separate for maximum air-cooling effect. The crankcases were split diagonally and primary drive was by chain. The cylinders were 51 × 60 mm in dimension and the 490 cc produced a reputed 26/28 bhp at 6000 rpm. The likelihood is that a solitary engine was built for bench testing,

whereupon, inexplicably, the project was allowed to lie dormant for a couple of years.

In 1927 Bonmartini and a like-minded peer, Count Lancelotti, injected capital into a new engineering company called OPRA (Officina Precisione Romana Automobili), and grander premises, equipped with quality precision machines, were acquired off via Ostiense. Remor and Gianini seem to have experimented with a variety of GRB-based engines during the year. Contemporary reports suggest that on one version an sohc assembly was run by a central gear train, replacing the previous shaft, while a second engine probably retained the shaft drive but was fitted with a twin-cam head. Other variants may have been produced. The one constant feature on the multi was the use of air-cooling which, so the engineers boasted, was as efficient as any water-cooling system.

By 1928 the engine had been perfected and a rudimentary frame built to house it; the team now sought out a rider. Piero Taruffi stepped on

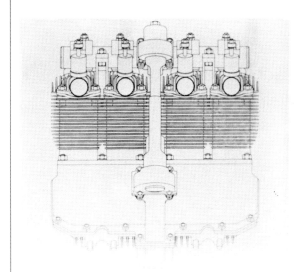

Air-cooled GRB four-cylinder engine of the mid-1920s

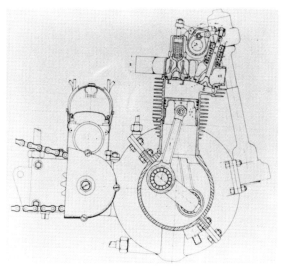

GRB measured 51 × 60 mm for a capacity of 490 cc

to the stage. Another Roman, born in 1906, Taruffi had recently completed his engineering studies and, encouraged by his father, was a prominent contender in national events on his home-tuned 500 cc Norton. With rare riding ability combined with mechanical expertise, Taruffi was an ideal development rider and was invited to undertake the first test runs of the OPRA on via Salaria.

Taruffi still remembers the bike clearly: 'The cooling system was a mixture of air and water; the cylinders were air-cooled but the head was jacketed with a little radiator in front of the petrol tank.' Evidently, the team's faith in the efficacy of the previous air-cooling system had not been entirely justified. The engine had assumed its final form, with which Taruffi was familiar; he recalls it clearly: 'I only ever saw one engine, which had twin cams run by a central gear train running off the central flywheel. The four cylinders were cast in monobloc form, with detachable heads.' The two valves per cylinder were of large diameter and set at 90 degrees within the hemispherical heads. Power was in the range 32 to 34 bhp at 7000 rpm, which was a phenomenal figure for the period and almost 10 bhp up on many rivals, and the compression ratio was recorded at 6:1. Contrary to Taruffi's fears, he found that the prototype racer was surprisingly sleek, with an unexpectedly narrow engine which did not protrude beyond the footrests.

Apart from the revolutionary engine, the OPRA was conventional with a double-loop frame, a magneto sitting atop the separate three-speed gearbox, chain primary and final drive, exhaust pipes which merged into one on each side and an oil tank placed beneath the saddle. Stopping the machine was effected by the dubious means of a crude friction brake working on a rim attached to the spokes.

The initial test session was hair-raising. Timing was primitive: two men with handkerchiefs stood a kilometre apart, while one man was placed in the middle with a stop-watch. This crude system recorded the OPRA's speed as 106 mph, against the 100 mph that Taruffi could register on his currently unassailable Norton. The tests came to an unscheduled conclusion when a tyre stripped, wrapping itself between the front forks and mudguard but fortunately not locking the wheel. After zigzagging for over 200 yards, Taruffi calmly dismounted and pronounced himself distinctly impressed with the racer.

Deeming the machine raceworthy, Bonmartini entered it for Rome's Royal GP over 20 laps of the Three Fountains circuit, a twisting eight-mile course, ill-suited to the characteristics of the potent OPRA. For the bike's début, the OPRA management determined on maximum publicity and so, to the chagrin of the relatively unknown Taruffi, hired the experienced Umberto Faraglia, a former Italian champion.

Faraglia lined up against the cream of Italy's riders: the ever-elegant Achille Varzi in check plus-fours, the scruffy Nuvolari with a spare chain hanging around his neck and Pietro Ghersi on his Sunbeam. This formidable array of talent was immediately left floundering by the rapid OPRA, but after three laps the riled Taruffi, using the superior handling of his English mount to best advantage, swept into a lead which he was not to relinquish. The OPRA blew up in vain pursuit.

Taruffi's run of success in 1928, eight victories from nine starts and the national 500 cc championship, convinced the OPRA staff that he was their man for the forthcoming season. Unfortunately, he was to be restricted to a solitary appearance on the bike in 1929, at the Belfiore circuit in Mantua. He led without challenge until the penultimate lap, when a rod went through the side, cancelling his efforts.

Taruffi recalls that the team was discouraged by this setback and the bike was put to one side in the workshop. He remembers his partnership with the two engineers with no little pride: 'Remor was a brilliant mathematician and Gianini was very creative. Together they could solve any theoretical problem, whereas I was just an amateur. But they badly needed someone with practical experience and ability, someone to ride the bike to the limit, and that was where I came in. I think that they formed the most complete team I ever worked with.' High praise indeed from a man whose career subsequently embraced spells with Enzo Ferrari's équipe and the mighty Mercedes organization. But the partnership was disbanded in 1929, never to re-form, as Taruffi reverted to his faithful Norton and an increasing involvement in car racing.

Unbeknown to Taruffi, there was a postscript to the OPRA story when the bike was resurrected in 1930. In May of that year it took its last bow, again at the Royal GP, before a massive crowd, including *il Duce*'s sons, Bruno and Vittorio. The OPRA was maintaining a respectable second place, behind eventual winner Mario Colombo (Sunbeam), when it blew up at half-distance. Sadly, the scribes of the time did not see fit to record the name of the rider of the ill-starred machine. Bonmartini did now lose patience and offered the design for sale. The French firm Gnome et Rhone made an enquiry, but, fortunately for Gilera, nothing came of it.

On the international front, the multi had seemingly made little advance by 1930; in Manxland, the Senior TT had fallen to Rudge, thanks to Walter Handley, and the same marque powered Terzo Bandini to that season's Italian title. But changes were in the air, for the supercharger was coming into prominence, and this device was almost literally breathing new life into the multis. In Germany, the BMW concern, planning a series of speed record attempts with its horizontally-opposed twins, had taken advantage of a blower designed by the Swiss engineer Zoller. This used four sliding vanes and was placed between the carburettor and the induction manifold, so that the mixture could be pumped into the combustion chamber at more than atmospheric pressure, thus exploding more air and fuel and producing more power. Crucially, a multi, with its more frequent supply

of intake strokes, was better suited than a single to use with a supercharger. In Italy, the engineers of Moto Guzzi soon latched on to this principle and fitted a vane-type Cozette blower to their new four-cylinder engine, which produced a healthy 45 bhp. Regrettably, the frame was not as sophisticated as the power-plant so that the Mandello racer never took to the tracks in anger. Nevertheless, the moral was clear: whoever could harness a supercharger to a multi would be on to a sure-fire winner.

In the early 1930s the Fascist bureaucracy, as part of its image-building procedure, was busy promoting the Italian aviation industry with its overtones of modernity, glamour and military might. So it was that for some years Bonmartini's considerable energies were channelled into establishing yet another new aircraft company that he had formed: CNA (Compagnia Nazionale Aeronautica). Gianini was retained to design experimental plane engines, including an ambitious X-12, whereas, according to Taruffi, Remor fell into dispute with his overlord and thereafter sought fresh employment. Evidence of Remor's argumentative nature surfaced with remarkable consistency over the next 20 years.

Fortunately, Bonmartini's sporting instincts remained intact. The company's premises were near the Littorio airport on the outskirts of Rome and were surrounded by the track of that name. The Littorio circuit on occasion hosted the Italian GP and enabled Bonmartini to test his racing Alfa as he pleased on a first-class track. In 1933 the Count, with recharged commitment, set about assembling staff to help Gianini resuscitate the lapsed OPRA project. A Roman engineer, Luigi Fonzi, was brought in as draughtsman. Taruffi, who had been riding a Norton and driving an Alfa for Scuderia Ferrari, was invited to act as Gianini's assistant and rider on a part-time basis.

The CNA racing motorcycle was designed in 1933. The supercharged engine, although loosely based on the OPRA in that it was a transverse four-cylinder affair, owed very little to its

Above **The CNA Rondine of 1935**

Below **Ciceroni, Taruffi and Rossetti on the starting grid for the Tripoli GP. Note the Rondine's dolphin fairing**

predecessor. The frame was also to be novel, although it borrowed some English design principles. Taruffi was an ardent admirer of the roadholding of his Norton, which was dismantled in the CNA workshop, where its principal features, such as wheelbase and the angle of the steering head, were measured ready for transplantation to the new frame.

The machine was prepared for testing early in 1934 and was dubbed the Rondine (swallow) by Bonmartini. Alas, Taruffi then crashed an experimental Maserati in the Tripoli GP lottery race. He lay in hospital for three months, enduring endless skin grafts on his seriously injured legs, while, to Taruffi's frustration, the initial tests were carried out by Bonmartini. As the engine was found to be producing 60 bhp at 8500 rpm, undreamt-of figures, it was necessary to recruit the Roman rider Amilcare Rossetti for the more searching test sessions.

The Rondine made its début on 31 March 1935, at, ironically, the Tripoli GP. Arriving at the Mellaha circuit, Taruffi found that the bend at which he had come to grief a year before had been renamed in his honour. Rossetti also travelled to the Italian colony to partner him.

The transverse four-cylinder CNA engine retained the dohc mechanism of the OPRA but otherwise had been completely redesigned. The cylinders, now each of 52×58 mm, sloped forwards at 45 degrees to allow a supercharger to sit above the crankcase. Designed largely by Taruffi, the supercharger was unusual in that it employed a meshing pair of three-lobe rotors, common enough in the four-wheeled sport, instead of the vanes favoured by motorcycle engineers. There were two castings of two cylinders each, although Taruffi recalls that the foundry work was complicated as the heads were integral. The two valves per cylinder, set at 90 degrees, used coil springs. The inlet camshaft drove both the rev counter and the water pump. The cylinders were entirely water-cooled, with the radiator above the heads, merging neatly into the lines of the tank. The crankshaft was a delicate built-up affair, using loose rollers, which would irritate the mechanics by failing after a mere 200 miles.

The integral four-speed gearbox was of novel CNA design, being semi-automatic so that changes could be made without using the multiple-disc clutch. At this point it is worth dispelling one long-standing myth. It has generally been reported by British journalists, although not by their Italian counterparts, that the primary gear drive of the Rondine and its Gilera progeny was taken from the middle of the crankshaft, from between cylinders two and three. This mistake, commonly made in books and articles, probably originated in a translation error in 1937 and seems to have been slavishly repeated since then. The truth was that although gear drive to the twin cams was indeed central, that to the gearbox and the blower was taken from between cylinders one and two on the Rondine and subsequently on the Gilera. There is also evidence that the primary transmission was on occasion taken from between cylinders three

and four, but, as will be seen, this is less compelling. It is, however, undeniable that it was the CNA engine which spawned the classic transverse four copied so successfully by MV, Honda and a plethora of worthy imitators. Traditionally, credit as father of the four has been accorded to Remor; in justice, judgement should be revised in favour of Gianini and Taruffi.

The unusual frame consisted of pressed-steel sections which ran from the steering head down to engine mountings on each side of the crankcase in line with the crankshaft, from there to the rear axle and thence directly back to the steering head, forming a stiff triangulated assembly. Other features were drum brakes, a large oil tank beneath an elongated saddle, a vertical magneto above the gearbox—although coil ignition was also tried—and a single vertical spring in front of the steering head. A revolutionary aspect of the two bikes that appeared in Tripoli was a fairing, in dolphin mode, witness to Taruffi's abiding concern for windcheating.

The 1935 Tripoli GP, an event stage-managed as a tribute to Fascist efficiency, enjoyed the latest time-keeping facilities, ultra-modern stands and pits in gleaming white concrete and a picturesque setting amidst palm trees—all strangely at odds with the informal practising along open roads along which a motley collection of peasants, camels and donkeys journeyed. The race was to signal the début not only of the CNA team but also of the new Benelli single in the hands of Guglielmo Sandri and the revised Guzzi V-twin, which was now equipped with rear suspension.

A bizarre incident preceded the race. Stanley Woods had been allowed to practise, but it was discovered that his entry had not been received by the organizing club. Indeed, the completed forms were later found languishing in the Guzzi offices. On the evening preceding the race, a perturbed Woods and Giorgio Parodi, one of the founders of the Mandello concern, dined with

Taruffi riding to victory at Pescara on the Rondine, now shorn of its fairing

the Governor of the colony, Italo Balbo, who reassured them that all would be well. However, Bonmartini, ignoring pleas that Woods had travelled from Ireland for the event, lodged a protest which he refused to withdraw even as the machines were assembling on the starting grid. Thus humiliated, in a mighty tantrum, Balbo threw away the flag and stormed off, leaving a minor dignitary to start the race. Woods, although relegated to the unaccustomed role of spectator, later confessed that he had been impressed by the determined manner with which Bonmartini had withstood not-so-petty officialdom. Unfortunately for the Count, the tale had an unsavoury sequel some months later.

In the race, the four remaining Guzzis, led by the fiery Omobono Tenni, increased the lap record from 100 mph to 108 mph in their frenzied attempts to pull away from Taruffi. They overstretched themselves in the process and blew up, leaving Taruffi and Rossetti to take first and second places: an unblemished début.

The CNA squad did not rest on its laurels. A duplex tubular frame was built in light alloy, although it was not destined to be raced. In readiness for the next appearance, the Coppa Acerbo in Pescara, Taruffi, never too proud to acknowledge another's bright idea, introduced a friction-damped pivoted rear-springing system, blatantly inspired by that pioneered by Carlo Guzzi on his wide-angle twin.

Stung by their unwelcome reverse in Tripoli, Guzzi added Giordano Aldrighetti and Terzo Bandini to their riding forces, while CNA retaliated by signing Sandri and Carlo Fumagalli. The three Rondine machines, although shorn of their fairings at Pescara, were armed with over 60 bhp and proved too much of a handful for the Guzzis, endowed with a comparatively modest 44 bhp. Timed over a flying kilometre, the day's fastest speeds were Sandri at 133 mph, Taruffi with 128 mph, Fumagalli at 125 mph and, in a remote fourth, Tenni's 120 mph. Such a decisive advantage more than compensated for the Rondine's apparent handling deficiencies; indeed, one rider dubbed it a camel, and at perhaps 340 lb it must have been some 20 lb heavier than the Mandello challenger. After Sandri suffered carburettor problems which relegated him to third spot, Taruffi took the flag, a convincing winner from Tenni.

At the end of May came the CNA's final race appearance at Monza in the Italian GP, which had been reduced to national status. *Il Duce*'s territorial ambitions were currently centred on hapless Ethiopia and rendered international relations rather fragile. Nevertheless, all the Italian works teams were assembled. The Guzzi équipe had its comprehensive revenge with Bandini, Tenni and Aldrighetti making a clean sweep of the rostrum positions. Taruffi's engine would not function and he was constrained to retire. Rossetti, restored to the team, had carburation problems, as did Carlo Fumagalli, who nevertheless managed to limp home a distant fifth, with the scant consolation of the record lap at 107 mph.

The racing career of the Rondine was now inexplicably cut short, but there was an epilogue

Taruffi aboard the Rondine in its record-breaking guise in November 1935

in November when the team travelled to the Firenze–Mare *autostrada* for an assault on speed records. Gianini and Taruffi appreciated that

aerodynamic drag was a crucial factor in this context and fitted the machine with a fairing more complete than that which had been employed in Tripoli. Although the front wheel remained uncovered, the fairing extended beneath the engine and a long tail was added, so that the machine was virtually fully enclosed apart from slots for the rider's legs. After two days of testing, the squad decided to go for the records at dawn when the air was still. Taruffi warmed the bike up, had the plugs changed by head mechanic Soderini and was ready to embark on his attempt when Bonmartini strode along, togged up in full kit, and commandeered the machine, anxious to grab some personal glory, much to the evident displeasure of Taruffi's father.

Predictably, at about 120 mph, Bonmartini lost control. He was flung down the road for almost 200 yards, performing three somersaults but sustaining no serious injuries. A couple of days later, with the repaired cowling around a spare frame, Taruffi captured the flying kilometre and mile records for the 500 cc class at 152 mph, the first of many world records he was to collect.

At this stage, the nefarious Italo Balbo re-entered the saga. He was now running the aviation ministry and was taking the opportunity to make life difficult for CNA in retribution for the Tripoli episode. Discouraged, Bonmartini decided to retire and sold his business to the Caproni aeroplane organization of Milan. Included in the deal, no doubt as an afterthought, was the Rondine motorcycle package. After 12 years in Rome, the transverse four-cylinder engine was moving north and to a new chapter in its history.

3 European assault

Team leader Giordano Aldrighetti pictured in 1938

1936–37

Although the Caproni company was subsequently to commence motorcycle production with a range of lightweight models, in 1936 Gianni Caproni's priorities were with aircraft manufacture. Accordingly, he asked Taruffi to find a buyer for the unwanted racers. Taruffi had to look no further than the other side of Milan, where Giuseppe Gilera eagerly seized the gilt-edged opportunity to acquire a proven race winner with untapped potential.

As a term of the agreement, Gilera insisted that Taruffi should work for him. Taruffi recalls the reasons: 'Gilera was a talented mechanic and quite prepared to turn his hand to development, but he realized and accepted his limitations as an engineer. Therefore, he asked me to join him to develop the bike. So I left Rome and went to Arcore together with the six Rondine motorcycles which had been built, all the designs and spares, and one of the CNA mechanics, tiny Orlando Ciceroni, nicknamed Romanino, who was familiar with the machines.'

After the years of Bonmartini's benevolent amateurism, Taruffi now found himself under the regime of an equally enthusiastic but hard-nosed businessman, determined not to jeopardize the long-awaited prospects of top-level sporting success by indulging in half-measures. Gilera immediately ordered a complete revision of the basically sound CNA design in order to marry thus far elusive reliability to the evident speed.

His main cause for concern was the fragile crankshaft, which had a meagre racing life of one meeting, after which the main bearings would wear out, necessitating dozens of hours of painstaking rebuilding. Gilera was not prepared to tolerate the waste of the mechanics' labour involved in this procedure and gave Taruffi strict instructions to cure the defect, failing which he would cut his losses by closing the race shop.

Throughout 1936, Gilera and Taruffi worked together on the redesign. The crankshaft problem was solved by the adoption of roller bearings with duralumin cages, extending its life to 100 hours or a season's racing. Using the factory's latest precision tools, Taruffi refined the lobes of the Roots-type blower and provided more extensive finning for both the supercharger and its balance chamber, which matched the supercharger's delivery to the engine's demand.

In the interests of handling, the sheet-steel frame was discarded in favour of a tubular-steel version, still with the same triangular shape for rigidity and a low centre of gravity. The Rondine's pressed-steel front forks were retained, with a single spring and friction dampers. At the rear, a suspension peculiar to Gilera was introduced. As early as 1934, Gilera had fitted his trials bikes with a triangulated swinging fork controlled by springs carried in horizontal tubes running above wheel spindle height. This system, equipped with massive hand-adjusted friction dampers, was now transplanted to the racers. In an age when the sceptical and less adventurous toyed with plunger-type rear springing, the Gilera system was way in advance of its contemporaries, other than that of the perennial rival Guzzi, which actually was even more sophisticated, for the triangulation and springing were below pivot height on the Mandello racers, thus lowering the centre of gravity.

Other features of the new Gilera were light-alloy wheels fitted with 3 × 21 in. and 3.50 × 20 in. tyres front and rear, single-leading-shoe brakes disposed to the right, a dry clutch with gear selection by a huge heel-and-toe rocking pedal on the right, a Weber carburettor, a Bosch vertical magneto above the gearbox and rev-counter drive from the exhaust camshaft. The triangular petrol tank, which contained 22 litres, was finished in dark red and the cycle parts were black. The new bikes evolved from the Rondine machines which, according to Taruffi, were butchered to provide the common parts. The only retrograde step was that a separate saddle and mudguard pad replaced the Rondine's elongated saddle. Weight was in the region of 350 lb and Taruffi estimated that initially power was about 70 bhp at 8800 rpm, which, if some 10 bhp down on Gilera's more extravagant claims, was a significant improvement on the CNA's output and way ahead of the opposition. In tests, Taruffi squeezed 137 mph out of an unfaired model.

Giuseppe Gilera proposed to dip his toe into the international waters in 1937 for an experimental season and signed up a top-flight rider in the Milanese jockey Giordano Aldrighetti, a noted stylist who had been Italian 500 cc champion in 1933 on one of Enzo Ferrari's Rudges.

In the early season curtain-raiser from the head to the heel of Italy, the inaugural Milano–Taranto, or the Coppa Mussolini as the event had been tactfully dubbed, Aldrighetti arrived fifth in Taranto, well down on Sandri's victorious V-twin Guzzi but in ample vindication of the crankshaft redesign.

At the beginning of July, the new team made its international début at the Bremgarten Forest circuit in Berne, the scene of the Swiss GP and host to that year's European GP. Aldrighetti and Taruffi lined up with another 20 starters for 45 laps of the tricky $4\frac{1}{2}$-mile course, which undoubtedly favoured the better-handling un-blown models. Gilera's entry into the GP fray had a slapstick aura, reminiscent of George Formby's hapless start on his Rainbow in the TT depicted in the timeless film *No Limit*. In his enthusiasm,

Aldrighetti accelerated off the start line only to shunt Noel Pope's Norton, fall off and hit Norton's maestro Joe Craig, innocently standing by the side of the track. Despite this mayhem, Aldrighetti remounted and caught the leaders, only to retire after a paltry six laps. A similar fate befell Taruffi, leaving Jimmy Guthrie to claim the European title, being decided on the outcome of one race for the last time.

At the end of the month, both Gilera riders led but retired at the Rome GP, an Italian championship race whereat Sandri registered yet another success en route to the season's national title. Discouraged, the Gilera team withdrew its entries from the ill-starred German GP, which was marred by Guthrie's fatal accident just before the chequered flag.

In August, the squad regrouped for the Swedish GP at the fast Saxtorp circuit near Malmo. Luigi Gilera was on hand to oversee mechanics Ciceroni and Ferruccio Colucci, who cared for the two machines. Aldrighetti and Taruffi encouragingly set the fastest practice times, but an embarrassing incident caused them to threaten to withdraw. The race programmes referred to the bikes as 'Gilera-Rondine'. Whatever the rights and wrongs of this nomenclature, which has persisted to this day, the Arcore équipe would have none of it, insisting to organizers and journalists alike that the machines were of exclusively Gilera manufacture and should be described accordingly. By perverse coincidence, *Motor Cycling*'s report stated that both Gilera motorcycles had been built as a hobby in the machine shops at Rome Airport!

Despite the unholy commotion and wrangles, both machines, predictably enough, duly took their allotted places at the head of the starting grid. As at Berne, a tiny screen was fitted, but Taruffi now experimented with two side springs on the front forks rather than the customary central spring. Incessant rain before the race left the course both damp and muddy, but,

undeterred, Aldrighetti established a 20-second lead over the BMWs of Otto Ley and Karl Gall after only four of the 26 laps. At this point, a blockage in the petrol feed brought the Milanese rider to a permanent halt. The BMW duo had probably been sounding out the Gilera's potential, for thereafter they upped the pace at will, even though unchallenged. After 2½ hours' racing, Ley pipped his compatriot by a meagre tenth of a second. Taruffi inherited a fortunate third place when Ragnar Sunnqvist, the idol of the 115,000-strong crowd, suffered a cracked head on his raucous DKW. The Gilera development rider, plagued by a persistent misfire, took the flag over six minutes behind the rampant BMW pair. With this rostrum position, Piero Taruffi's illustrious motorcycling racing career came to an end.

A couple of weeks later, in a sizzling Italian GP at Monza, the team came of age. Aldrighetti's machine did enjoy one modification for the event. It was clothed in a partial fairing, which was little more than an extended leg shield, and nothing like as comprehensive as the Rondine's cowling. Nevertheless, Aldrighetti estimated that it was good for another 5 mph in top speed, which was at a premium over the royal parkland track. The Gilera number one was left to fend for himself as early as the fourth lap, when new team-mate Ettore Villa retired, but, in company with Gall on the potent German twin, he soon blasted ahead of the pack. To the immense disappointment of the fiercely partisan multitudes, Aldrighetti lost half a minute when refuelling. By dint of constantly breaking the lap record—finally leaving the lap speed at 111 mph, a 5 mph improvement on the previous best—he established a 40-second lead over Omobono Tenni. Aldrighetti was then obliged to pull into his pit once more to change a plug, relinquishing the lead. Undaunted, in another inspired bout he caught the Guzzi demon and took the chequered flag 18 seconds ahead of his rival, with Sandri, Gall, Woods and Ley in his wake. He

The supercharged four-cylinder Gilera in its 1938 format. Note the tubular frame, abbreviated fairing and unusual rear suspension

toured in to tumultuous applause from the assembled throng, having recorded the first, and one of the most stunning, of Gilera's Grand Prix victories.

Thus, Gilera's preliminary season in Grand Prix racing, despite its intermittent setbacks, concluded with a resounding performance which augured well for the forthcoming campaign.

1938

Due to his commitment to four-wheeled sport, Taruffi regretfully came to the conclusion that he

no longer had the time to race the Gilera. However, he remained employed by the factory in his elevated role of team manager, in which capacity he sought out a replacement rider. His choice fell on the personable Dorino Serafini, a pocket battleship of a racer and the inseparable friend of Aldrighetti since 1932, when their careers blossomed on 175 cc Benelli machines. More than team harmony and sentiment dictated the choice. Born in 1909 in Pesaro, the self-styled 'Home of Italian Motorcycling', Serafini had collected a national title in 1933 on a 175 cc MM and had repeated the achievement three years later in the blue-riband class on a single-cylinder 500 cc Bianchi. As back-up for the Italian races, Taruffi selected Francesco Lama from Faenza. Lama's foremost claim to celebrity was victory in the 175 cc class of the Italian GP at the Littorio circuit in 1933, again on an sohc MM, the product of Mario Mazzetti's partnership with his more renowned colleague Alfonso Morini.

The motorcycle was tidied up for the impending season. A tiny fairing, more of a leg shield really, sprouted out of the downtubes, which had been flattened at their lower ends in order to form engine mountings in imitation of the Rondine. Still concerned with streamlining, Taruffi fashioned a half-moon-shaped rear mudguard, incorporating the oil tank beneath the saddle.

The domestic season began encouragingly enough when Aldrighetti covered the daunting 769 miles over open roads from Milan to Taranto at a record speed of 73 mph to win the Coppa

Mussolini. Both Serafini and Lama retired. Serafini recollects that the riders had orders from Taruffi not to take the engine beyond 7000 rpm, but, if asked to do so, it would operate at 8000 rpm all day long. After the race, Aldrighetti confessed to Serafini that he had indeed asked and the engine had not failed him.

Three weeks later, in the second championship event at Bologna, Aldrighetti was first and Lama second. Next, on to the Turin GP, where the team leader guaranteed himself the title with

Dorino Serafini in the paddock for the 1938 German GP

his third consecutive victory, this time shadowed by Serafini. In the fourth and final round over the imposing Lario course, Aldrighetti led only to retire, handing the victory to Serafini, who, now becoming accustomed to the characteristics of the supercharged multi, broke both lap and race records.

The team's preoccupation with the Italian races necessitated missing both the TT and the Belgian GP, the first two of the season's events which were qualifying rounds of the redesigned European championship, to be decided on a points system rather than the outcome of one race. The Gilera riders opened their international account at the Swiss TT at the Berne circuit in early July, which, not being part of the title series, attracted a predominantly non-works entry. Aldrighetti and Serafini were patently faster than the motley opposition, but both retired, enabling the Swiss Georges Cordey on his private Norton to record a popular victory. Worse was to befall the duo two weeks later at the classic Swiss GP on the notorious Geneva street circuit with its hazardous tram-lines and ramps. The race began in Serafini-induced chaos as he pushed off too early, causing the rest of the field to jump the start with him. At the end of the first lap of just two miles, the crowd was staggered as Serafini's red helmet appeared, followed by his team-mate, for they had already established a healthy lead of over 200 yards. The demonstration run came to a dramatic conclusion. On lap eight, when in a secure second place, Aldrighetti lost control as he crossed a tram-ramp and fell, suffering severe concussion and injuries which were to put him out of action for the remainder of the season. Only three laps later, with tears of frustration streaming down his face, a disconsolate Serafini toured into the pits to retire with a puncture, thought to have been caused by the bike's terrific

Second-string Silvio Vailati, seen at Sachsenring in 1939

acceleration forcing the valve out. Norton's standard-bearer, the bespectacled Harold Daniell, thus added to his Senior TT victory with ease.

The circus, now minus the stricken Aldrighetti but plus BMW's Georg Meier, already with the Belgian GP to his credit, moved on to Assen for the Dutch TT. Serafini, now Gilera's sole representative, made a forlorn attempt to stay with the invincible blown German twins, but as he passed his pit for the fourth time, he made snaking signals. Sure enough, he came off next lap. Having remounted, he struggled to his pit, where he kicked the pedals back into shape while the mechanics reset the handlebars. To appreciative cheers, he set off and eventually finished a plucky third, behind BMW's second string, van Hammersveld, and with the indignity of having been lapped by the rampant Meier.

The next round was at Sachsenring, host to the European GP, where Serafini held Meier in the early stages until an oil leak gave a dangerous coating to the rear tyre and his boots, forcing him in to be cleaned up by Taruffi and refuelled by Ciceroni. His progress was subsequently terminated by a broken clutch wire and Meier romped home before 300,000 of his admiring countrymen.

Finally, at the end of September, came the most galling disappointment in the home GP at Monza. Serafini, having smashed the lap record, was forced to retire on the fourth lap with blower problems. Meier, confirming his new-found status as European champion, chalked up yet another victory, backed up by team-mate Kraus. Gilera's new reserve riders, Silvio Vailati and Carlo Fumagalli, who had ridden the Rondine three years earlier, were roundly beaten into third and fourth places respectively.

Despite the disastrous Grand Prix showing, Serafini was far from downhearted. First and foremost for a professional rider, he was well paid, receiving 2000 lire a month which was ten times his former Bianchi salary, together, of course, with all expenses. Additionally, the factory would match any prize money he won. His contract did not, however, allow him to retain any trade sponsorship; that was to be allocated to the team's running expenses.

Furthermore, he was at ease with his colleagues: 'Taruffi, although perhaps not an absolutely top-flight rider like Aldrighetti, was an extremely thorough organizer and team manager; Ciceroni was a meticulous mechanic and Luigi Gilera was a wonderfully affable companion in our travels over Europe, ever ready for a drink and a caper. Giuseppe Gilera was rather more formal, but he was a gentleman and always treated his riders with respect. Indeed, my only problem with him was that he was reluctant to let me test the bikes at full speed. He would order me not to take unnecessary risks, whereas I wanted to test the bikes under racing conditions. The only real difficulty I had within the team, following Aldrighetti's departure and as my results improved, was with the other riders.'

Finally, Serafini had the utmost faith in the bike. He recollects: 'It was by far the best I ever rode. Although it was heavier than, say, a Norton or a Velocette, which were like bicycles in comparison, that was no particular disadvantage because the Gilera was, after development, very stable, as long as the rider was strong enough to hold it. As for the engine, not only was it the most powerful of its day, it was virtually indestructible. In tests at Monza, and indeed in the Milano–Taranto, it could be over-revved for hours on end without complaint. Although we suffered too many frustrating retirements in 1938, I cannot remember the engine blowing up. Our retirements were down to niggling, irritating mistakes; for example, in the German GP one of the mechanics did not tighten up a cap properly, causing oil to drench my tyre, and so on.'

Ciceroni and Serafini waiting for the start of the 1939 German GP

Thus, although 1938 had not been the unqualified success the team had been hoping for, Serafini remained optimistic as the new season dawned. His confidence was to prove well founded; his loyalty was to be amply rewarded.

1939

As 1939 unwound, the Gilera was in essence little changed from the Rondine designed five years before. The basic features were retained: a duplex triangular frame and the pressed-steel girder forks with friction dampers; the two valves per cylinder sitting in a perfectly hemispherical combustion chamber; the twin cams, driven by a central gear train; a gear-driven integral four-speed gearbox; each pair of exhaust pipes joined below the crankcase, with single pipes on each side terminating in a very shallow megaphone. Over the years, Gilera had done little more than tinker with Gianini's creation: their own rear suspension system had been engrafted; the crankshaft, running on six main bearings, had been strengthened; an enormous crankcase breather sprang up, and the bike's aerodynamics had been tidied up.

The restless Taruffi was not content and now made a number of further modifications. The radiator was fitted with a set of shutters for use in cold weather, while circulation was improved by the use of a revised water pump driven from the inlet camshaft. Ribbed side panels appeared on the oil tank, from which sprouted two breather pipes that merged in the tail and protruded from the rear of the mudguard. Finally, on a bike built halfway through the season, the frame was revised in that the rear forks, from the engine mountings back, reverted to the Rondine's pressed-steel arrangement.

The engine, with a compression ratio of 8:1, had been refined to produce about 75 bhp, sufficient to propel the 350 lb bike to 145 mph. For illuminating comparisons, it is worth noting that at the 1939 TT, Meier's BMW, Daniell's

Norton and Rusk's four-cylinder AJS weighed in at 302 lb, 332 lb and 404 lb respectively, while their power outputs were probably of the order of 68 bhp, 50 bhp and 70 bhp. There are, however, lies, damned lies, statistics and bhp claims. Velocette's presiding genius, Harold Willis, doubted whether the Gilera was churning out more than 50 bhp in reality. Be that as it may, the Arcore multi was undeniably some 5 mph faster than its supercharged rivals and 10–15 mph up on the unblown singles.

Taruffi's attention was also engaged by Aldrighetti's decision to forsake the team. The former number one rider was a talented all-round sportsman, having previously excelled at both ice hockey and football, and, completely recovered from his Geneva injuries, he determined to concentrate henceforth on driving an Alfa Romeo for Enzo Ferrari. Although Aldrighetti, being a Milanese, had been the acknowledged maestro and local favourite, Taruffi had every confidence in Serafini as his principal jockey. Taruffi recalls his qualities: 'He was extremely likeable, modest, easy-going and popular within the team. His engaging personality did, however, hide a firm inner conviction in his own boundless ability.'

There was no shortage of applicants for the team's vacancy, one of whom was future Ferrari world champion Alberto Ascari, who had been Serafini's replacement at Bianchi and now pestered Taruffi incessantly. The team manager instead confirmed Silvio Vailati as number two rider; he was the son of Ernesto Vailati, a Sunbeam rider and agent who had been one of Giuseppe Gilera's adversaries in the early days. The more experienced Carlo Fumagalli may have lost out because he and Serafini had been involved in an unseemly squabble over prize money during a season together at Bianchi: financial disputes cropped up in the sport long before the days of cigarette company mega-sponsorship. Francesco Lama was retained for the Italian events.

The 1939 Gilera—this one is Vailati's mount, pictured in the Sachsenring pits

Again the appearances of the four-cylinder models were to be restricted to the Italian and European title events. Serafini explains: 'Giuseppe Gilera was anxious that we should take these championships and would not allow us to jeopardize our chances by riding in minor national races, hillclimbs and the like.'

Serafini suffered his customary wretched luck in the curtain-raiser to the Italian championship, the Milano–Taranto. He had pulverized Aldrighetti's records for the stages when, within a few miles of Taranto, a wheel came off, causing him to hit the deck at over 120 mph. Miraculously unscathed, he hopped on to the back of a lorry and arrived in Taranto in time to welcome home the winner, team-mate Ettore Villa on one of the Gilera production racers, the eight-bolt model. Serafini takes up the tale: 'Of course, Villa thought that I had won and was pulling his leg until I explained that as I had had an hour's lead when I crashed, it was easy enough to reach the finishing line before him.'

Serafini made no mistake in the second championship round in May, winning at Foggia, with Lama in second place. Next month, Vailati pocketed the Bologna round. Unfortunately the final race coincided with the Dutch TT; Giuseppe Gilera decided that the European title was his priority and packed Serafini and Vailati off to Assen. Nevertheless, Lama won at Faenza and thereby, with his second place at Foggia, retained the national title for the team. Francesco Lama passed into semi-retirement after the war. His final appearance was at the Italian GP in 1948, when he gave the celebrated 125 cc Mondial its début, taking the lead and establishing the fastest lap over the Faenza circuit before retiring. He died in 1968, aged only 59.

For the assault on the European series, Taruffi's planning was comprehensive and meticulous. First, he devised new race tactics. In 1938, Aldrighetti and Serafini had pressed ahead regardless, showing their hand to the opposition, breaking lap records at random, only for some trifling gremlin to set in and permit the BMWs to pick up the pieces. Taruffi therefore determined on a cagey game plan and instructed Serafini to shadow the likely principal opponent, presumed to be Meier, until half-distance and then to increase the tempo if necessary.

Second, he saved valuable time during practice. The gear ratios for the races were established beforehand with the aid of a large-scale plan of each circuit. Taruffi outlines the technique: 'With a pair of compasses, I drew on the plan the arc of maximum radius that the Gilera could describe through each corner and I could then calculate the speed at which the bend could be taken. I knew the length of the straights and the bike's acceleration and so I could work out the maximum speed it would attain on the straights and could plot, with accuracy, the gear ratios. This saved us long-

Ciceroni, Vailati and Serafini salute the German GP triumph in the appropriate manner

winded, unproductive experiment once we arrived at the circuit.'

The team did not venture to Mona's Isle, where Meier, in the absence of pukka works Nortons, convincingly won the Senior TT. When the Italians belatedly began their campaign at Assen, Serafini sat menacingly on Meier's tail as ordered, with Vailati tucked in similarly behind BMW's second string, Kraus. In the Assen rain the two leaders weaved through the backmarkers until the half-distance pit stop, when slick work by his Teutonically efficient crew gave Meier a handy 12-second lead. With consummate ease, Serafini devoured the gap, passed Meier at will and was establishing an ever-increasing dominance when, on the penultimate lap, he fell on the curves at the back of the circuit. Undeterred, Serafini picked himself up and set off before Meier had time to catch him, only to fall a second time. This mishap was generally attributed to rider error and overenthusiasm, which Serafini disputes ardently: 'My goggles were bespattered with dirt thrown up off the damp track by the BMW, so I simply could not see where I was going.'

Only a lap from victory, he pulled into the pits for makeshift repairs, but an eagle-eyed official spotted the cracked handlebars and would not allow him to return to the fray. Meier, a little luckily, thus notched a fortunate Dutch TT win, his second victory of the new season, although Vailati salvaged some Italian pride with runner-up spot.

Both Gilera and BMW gave the French GP at Reims a miss and reappeared for the European GP at Spa. Taruffi, still obsessed with streamlining, took along a bike furnished with an eggshell-like fairing, based on that of a record-breaking model that he had campaigned in 1937. Taruffi had hoped that the fairing could be used to full advantage on the notoriously fast, scenic Ardennes circuit, but insufficient practice time meant that the bike never emerged from the team's van.

The Belgian GP did indeed turn out to be a high-speed trial, during which Meier attained 100 mph laps, the first to be registered in classic racing. Serafini, dutifully obeying team orders, held back, only to have his tactics rebound when he came upon a backmarker who stuck to the racing line at Spa's famous hairpin, causing the Italian to clout the straw bales as he scraped through a diminishing gap. More seriously, a rapid change-down had upset the gearbox, and so, when he stopped for refuelling and a chat with Taruffi, they decided that he should settle for a comfortable second spot. Indeed, he was lapped by his German rival who, now with three wins to his credit, seemed destined to retain his title.

Aldrighetti had been recalled to the team colours on a one-off basis and, although dropped by Meier and Serafini, he kept Kraus and Ginger Wood on the potent FN at bay, only to retire with engine trouble at three-quarters distance. He subsequently returned to Ferrari to drive in the Pescara GP, where he suffered fatal injuries in a practice smash. Peculiarly, the night before his death, he had slept in a hotel room numbered 17, a number traditionally considered unlucky by Italian racers.

Saxtorp, a flat course favouring top speed, was host to the Swedish GP and, at the eleventh hour, Taruffi's tactics paid off. Meier initially maintained a slender lead over Serafini, but only by dint of uncharacteristic excursions on to the grass verge, while further back Kraus went off the track in trying to fend off Vailati, now reinstated in the team. Meier, determined to win at all costs and displaying none of the eagerness to accumulate points which is such a prevalent feature of modern title bids, broke the lap record repeatedly in fruitless attempts to evade his pursuer. Journalists noted that the German was on the ragged edge, whereas Serafini was shadowing him with something in hand.

Sure enough, Meier eventually overdid it, going off on the same corner as his team-mate,

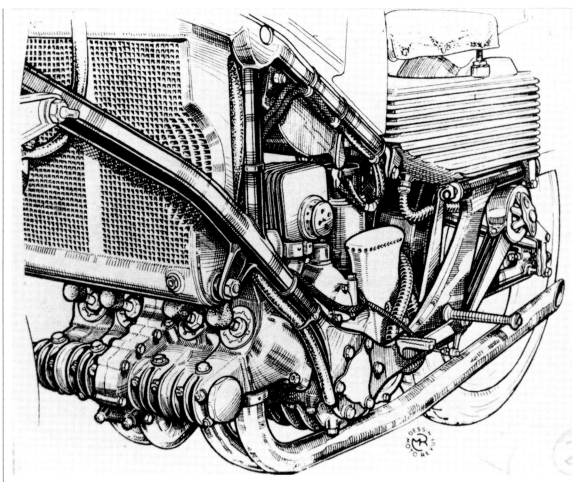

The 1939 Gilera, drawn in its final form. Note the use of pressed steel in the rear suspension

but, despite ending up in a ditch, he controlled his BMW and embarked on a pursuit of the Gilera. Having caught the Italian, Meier cast himself off the road yet again, this time injuring his back so severely that he would not ride again that season. Serafini rode to a clear victory, with Vailati second, well ahead of Kraus, whose third place was a phenomenal effort in view of the fact that his mishap had broken his leg.

At Sachsenring for its home Grand Prix, the BMW équipe found itself in unfamiliar chaos. Without the injured Meier and Kraus, the Munich firm called up novices Ruhrschneck and Lodermeier, who, unaccustomed to the peculiarities of the blown twin, could not ride it to its limit. Their team-mate, the veteran Mansfeld, evidently rode it beyond its limit and pranged twice in practice. Jock West, who had ridden the flat twin to two famous Ulster GP victories, was fortuitously in Bavaria on holiday and he was hastily summoned to the circuit to lead the German challenge. West performed admirably, holding Serafini until handling problems beset his machine, enabling the stocky Pesarese to coast to another unchallenged victory. Serafini had ridden the new bike with the revised frame, whereas Vailati had persevered with the tubular-framed model. Gilera's reserve rider was eventually forced out of the race by the pain of an injury sustained in practice.

Serafini was actually entered for the ISDT, which clashed with the Ulster GP, but as he was in with a golden chance of the title he was hustled off to Clady with the new bike. Serafini recalls that the one weakness of the 1939 model was its front brake: 'When racing with Meier, I was certainly faster but could not get away because my brakes were nothing like as efficient as the BMW's.' Accordingly, the updated machine was fitted with a full-width stronger front brake. In any event, the BMW squad were absentees; German industry had more imperative concerns as August deepened.

Taruffi noted that the British riders coped with the multitude of bumps on the demanding circuit not by thottling back but by lifting the handlebars and landing rear-wheel first. Serafini, with a heavier bike, could not manage this and was landing front-wheel first. This prompted a number of moments which the Italian mastered with a combination of strength and rare skill. Serafini, for his part, was rather amused at Gilera's tactics: 'They were quite cunning; with Vailati out, still injured, they decided not to provide a back-up rider. Their reasoning was that, on my own, I would ride responsibly and, to be fair, they were right because I rode well that day.'

The team did, however, make one tactical mistake, born out of understandable ignorance. It was decided that the greatest challenge was posed by Freddie Frith, and so, at flag fall, Serafini duly slotted in behind him. This policy took no account of the improvements made to the water-cooled AJS V4. This fearsome multi was ridden by the Ulsterman Walter Rusk, who immediately took command of his home GP and established the first three-figure lap of the Clady circuit at exactly 100 mph. Serafini recalls the performance: 'Rusk was thin, tall and very strong. Had he kept going, I think that he would have beaten me, not because his bike was faster than mine but because he was prepared to take more risks. I rode conservatively, whereas Rusk was riding over the edge. Down the Clady straight, I could see that the AJS was throwing him from side to side.' Once Rusk went out with a minor fork problem, Serafini's path was clear.

Serafini remembers the race's celebrated incident as he pulled level with Frith: 'I grinned at

Serafini riding to victory at the Ulster GP. Note the revised front brake on the updated model

him, and simply accelerated away into the lead. Frith was a fine rider, but he had absolutely no chance that day, so hopelessly underpowered was his Norton.' Frith regarded the incident as the most shattering experience of his career. Serafini went on to poach the lap record from Rusk with a tour at 100.03 mph. He also re-established the race as the world's fastest with a record of 97.85 mph, much to the satisfaction of the appreciative crowd, which gave him a tumultuous reception as the first foreign rider to win the Ulster Senior.

Unbeknown at the time, Serafini's third victory was sufficient to clinch the European title, for the proposed Swiss and Italian GPs were scrubbed following the outbreak of hostilities. Serafini eventually collected his cherished championship medal in 1949 and was honoured by the state in 1960 with the Italian equivalent of a knighthood.

Lest it be thought that Serafini collected the spoils simply thanks to the machine, the pertinent views of Guglielmo Sandri, the works Guzzi rider, should be aired. Sandri once opined that nobody ever raced a motorcycle with such conviction and authority as did Serafini in 1939; he also made the extravagant claim that on his day he was capable of mixing it with Tenni, Varzi and even the peerless Nuvolari, but he ruefully admitted that he was powerless against Serafini that season. As international racing ground to a halt, Serafini and the Gilera were firmly established at the top of the greasy pole.

Taruffi astride the record breaker after the sessions of April 1937—Ciceroni and Gilera can be seen to his right

Piero Taruffi's motorcycle racing career concluded in 1937 but his record-breaking exploits continued. He collected over 50 records on the Gilera

Mention should also be made of Piero Taruffi's record-breaking exploits on the blown Gilera. As early as 1936 Taruffi turned his attention to the 500 cc records that he had formerly claimed on the Rondine but which had been bettered by Ernst Henne's BMW, not to forget Eric Fernihough's 1000 cc Brough Superior. With the aid of the aerodynamic facilities in Caproni's aircraft factory, he designed an all-embracing aluminium shell which weighed 45 lb but was worth an extra 35 mph.

Taruffi decided against the complete fairing in favour of a version which did not enshroud the rider but which was designed to merge into the lines of his body. It was found that the bike became dangerously unstable at speeds in excess of 155 mph and so Taruffi added a fin to the top of the tail. This was dispensed with, as it rendered the machine oversensitive to cross-winds.

The record breaker had a longer frame than the racers, greater spring travel, no front brake and special tyres. The handlebars were shortened to fit inside the glass bubble; the loss of leverage encouraged wheel-wobble and so the steering damping was reinforced.

The first series of record attempts took place in April 1937, when the most notable achievement was the annexation of the classic hour record, which had stood to the credit of Jimmy Guthrie at 114 mph. Taruffi packed in 121 miles over a 28-mile course on the Bergamo to Brescia *autostrada*. At the Brescia end, there was no turning loop and the mechanics had to manhandle the bike to turn it around. Although hailed as a phenomenal performance, Taruffi modestly claimed that because of the machine's technical superiority, his had been a simple task. It has been reported that during this run Taruffi ran out of petrol and coasted a couple of miles to his crew; in fact, this mishap occurred during a practice run.

In October of that year came what Taruffi regarded as the greater test, when he tilted at Henne's 500 cc absolute record of over 169 mph. Taruffi practised on open roads and, satisfied that he could clip the record, he booked the *autostrada* for dawn, to avoid traffic and the wind. Using 10,250 rpm, Taruffi established a new record with a speed of 170.37 mph over the flying kilometre.

Finally, in April 1939, Taruffi upped the hour record, covering almost 127 miles in the 60 minutes. In all, he set over 50 records on the special Gilera. Serafini commented on his team manager's achievements in this sphere: 'As a racer, he was probably not quite in the top bracket like Aldrighetti, but as a record breaker he was unique, unrivalled, in both his preparation and his riding.'

Taruffi and Giuseppe Gilera in October 1937

4 | The home front

Although international competition inevitably ground to an enforced halt, a clash of giants was eagerly anticipated on the Italian tracks in 1940. For while *il Duce* dithered about committing himself alongside his belligerent Nazi pupil, the Italian clubs proposed 54 road races for the forthcoming season and the factories' enthusiasm for the fray continued unabated.

The Benelli concern from Pesaro plumped for a

Serafini (no. 6) on the starting grid for the Italian title race at Genoa in May 1940, which he won

supercharged four-cylinder 250 cc racer as its standard-bearer, but Bianchi and Guzzi were determined to tilt at Gilera's dominance in the half-litre class. Bianchi came up with a transverse four-cylinder vertical engine, employing Gilera dimensions of 52 × 58 mm, but the Milanese factory opted for air-cooling, while the dohc assembly was shaft-and-bevel-gear driven. The gear-driven, vane-type blower sat above the four-speed gearbox. The cycle parts were elementary; a simple tubular cradle frame, girder front forks and plunger rear suspension. Alberto Ascari tested the machine extensively at Monza, but it was never raced. Fortunately, an example survived the devastation inflicted on the factory during the war.

Theoretically, there was nothing about the Bianchi multi to cause Gilera undue concern; the frame and suspension were less sophisticated than those of the Arcore racer and its engine lagged four years behind in development. By contrast, Carlo Guzzi's new bike bristled with ingenious touches. His use of a supercharger, a gear-driven Cozette vane type similar to that already perfected on the marque's 250 cc single, was virtually mandatory, but his choice of an air-cooled three-cylinder engine was less predictable. The nearly-square cylinders (59 × 60 mm) were inclined forwards at 45 degrees like the Gilera, but the two valves per cylinder were governed by a twin-cam set-up driven by a chain, lurking behind a massive triangular cover on the right-hand side.

In time-honoured Guzzi tradition, particular attention was given to weight-saving. The engine-gearbox unit was mounted beneath an unusual spine frame formed from a combination of lightweight tubes at the top and pressed steel at the rear, without the customary downtubes. The Guzzi-designed triangulated rear swinging

fork controlled by horizontal springs came off the old V-twin, but, technically, was a match for the Gilera system. After winter test sessions, two novel features were incorporated: a five-speed gearbox and a twin-leading-shoe front brake.

Despite the evident menace, Gilera left their championship-winning model untouched. Piero Remor had just been brought to Arcore by Taruffi, primarily to produce the next generation 500 cc racer, but this task was delayed while Remor turned his mind to the design of a blown 250 cc machine. Serafini was not daunted by the failure to develop his bike: 'We had a head start over the opposition; the Gilera was both fast and reliable and we could afford to sacrifice a winter's development.' The first appearance of the team was at a non-championship shakedown in April at Alessandria, where Serafini, completely vindicated, rode to unchallenged victory.

The team's solitary problem arose from Serafini's complete domination of the scene. He explains: 'By now, Taruffi was having difficulty in recruiting a back-up rider. They all realized that I would win and so none of the riders wanted to join us.' This seemingly intractable poser plagued the squad during the Milano–Taranto saga in the middle of May. The 133 entrants started out from Milan at intervals of one minute. As Serafini was the last to start of the fancied Gilera runners, Taruffi gave instructions that his riders should not press the pace, so that the number one rider could pass by at his own speed, unhindered by his team-mates. A somewhat irked Silvio Vailati, also on a blown multi, would have none of this and set off at a searing tempo, forcing Serafini to ride hard. The European champion covered the 125 miles over open roads to Bologna at the record speed of 107.7 mph. Vailati was not far adrift, but third-place man Sandri on a 250 cc Guzzi was already out of touch.

When Serafini encountered chain trouble, Vailati inherited the lead. As in 1939, the flat-out pace eventually proved excessive for all the pukka works bikes. Both Vailati and Sandri

dropped out after Rome and Serafini, having struggled on, was unfortunately constrained to retire at virtually the same spot that had witnessed his spill the year before. Victory in the race of attrition went by default to Guido Cerato on a standard sports 500 cc Guzzi.

Guzzi unveiled the revolutionary triple in Genoa on 26 May for its first, and what turned out to be its final, appearance. Guglielmo Sandri was entrusted with the device at the Circuito del Lido di Albaro and it displayed a fair turn of speed, which impressed the assembled scribes. Indeed, perhaps optimistically, a power output of 80 bhp at 8000 rpm and a top speed of 135 mph were claimed, which were barely down on the Gilera. Be that as it may, Sandri soon had to pull into the pits for a plug change and he subsequently retired, leaving Serafini with yet another victory.

Serafini denied that the new Guzzi was a serious threat: 'The Gilera was much quicker. I was merely foxing with Sandri, testing him out. Had it become necessary, I could have left him readily enough.'

After the frustration of riding in Serafini's tracks and the difference of opinion with Taruffi over the Milano–Taranto tactics, Vailati switched his allegiance to the Guzzi camp to ride their blown quarter-litre model.

Mussolini was once described as a self-educated man who had a bad teacher and was a worse pupil. Within a matter of days of the Genoa meeting, he had opted to filch some of the crumbs from Herr Hitler's table and he plunged his forlorn nation into a miserable conflict. The British motorcycling press, far-sighted as ever, opined in Delphic fashion that the Italians had thereby deprived themselves of a marvellous opportunity to develop race-winning machinery.

The Gilera factory emerged unscathed from the war and the three supercharged solo racing bikes were intact. The team's personnel, however, required reconstruction. Taruffi de-

The supercharged multi, still in 1940 guise, pictured in the paddock at Geneva in 1946

cided to concentrate on car racing and left Arcore, albeit temporarily, with a tinge of bitterness. He explains: 'Remor eased me out because he did not want me around influencing Giuseppe. It certainly rankled with me; after all, Remor owed his job to me in the first place.'

Taruffi found some financial consolation; he was signed up by AMC's Jock West as agent for the Rome area. Serafini, who was an AMC agent for northern Italy, forsook motorcycles for a new lease of life on four wheels. His new career would embrace a works Ferrari drive and a runner-up

spot in the Mille Miglia of 1950, but was brought to an enforced conclusion by a serious accident in the following year's event which necessitated six or seven operations and left him with the legacy of a permanent limp.

The war-ravaged Italian factories were short of raw materials, and particularly tyres, but were nevertheless prepared to return to competition. The circus recommenced in January 1946 with a meeting in the suburbs of Rome. The organization was reported by the press to be disastrous, with a reference to the Marx brothers' performance in *Duck Soup* thrown in for good measure. The 500 cc event was won by a Gilera Saturno ridden by Bruno Francisci, who would feature again in the Arcore story. Undaunted by

Nello Pagani riding the blown multi to victory in the 1946 Swiss GP

this shambolic event and a chronic shortage of funds, the Italian clubs lined up 20 road-racing events. Gilera, although as ever pleading an acute lack of ready funds, determined to organize a team.

The experienced Nello Pagani was recruited as the new number one. Pagani had already been national 250 cc champion on three occasions and had ridden for Moto Guzzi before the war. After a falling out with the Mandello concern, he grasped the sought-after opportunity of a Gilera agency in Milan and a handsome retainer to race the multi. His back-up riders included Jader Ruggeri, the son of the pioneer Amadeo who had won the first Lario TT in 1921 aboard a Harley-Davidson. Amadeo's other son, Luigi, secured a works ride with Guzzi for 1946. Larger-than-life 30-year-old Carlo Bandirola was signed up to ride in the second, or junior, category.

The factories were thrown into disarray when the Italian federation decreed that superchargers would be outlawed henceforth in national events. Despite this edict, the era of the blown Gilera multi was not quite over.

Racing resumed in formerly neutral Switzerland with an open formula under which the use of blowers was permitted. The big race of the year, with its attendant publicity, was the GP over the Geneva circuit at the end of June. Pagani's Gilera, in the form raced by Serafini six years earlier, was the sole works entry, but his practice time was bettered by the Guzzi stalwart Enrico Lorenzetti. The event, held before 30,000 race-starved spectators, unwound in a predictable pattern; Pagani won much as he pleased, lapping second-place man Lorenzetti by the end of the 40 laps. At the beginning of September, Pagani took the blown machine just over the Swiss border and gave the famous racer its last victory at Mendrisio.

Guzzi, for one, now opted to discard their half-baked blown triple and wheel out their older singles and twins. The Mandello engineers appreciated that an engine designed to run with a blower would encounter severe carburation problems if shorn of its supercharger. For example, the AJS Porcupine, although it carried Les Graham to the world championship in 1949, was set down during the war as a blown engine and never ran smoothly once it had been modified.

Remor was set to work on a new 500 cc racer in 1946, but, as an interim measure, Gilera opted to revise two of their supercharged racers for the domestic season. The Roots-type blower was removed and replaced by two Weber carburettors, one for each pair of cylinders. A slightly enlarged petrol tank and a rear tyre measuring 3.50 × 20 in. were now featured. Although the machine had shed about 40 lb, this was insufficient to compensate for the hefty loss of power, which was cut to a modest 50 bhp. Top speed was reduced to about 135 mph, some 10 mph down on the 1940 version.

Despite the machine's inevitable carburation difficulties, Pagani notched up a couple of victories over local tracks before the first post-war Italian championship began. Out of the five 500 cc events, Pagani won at Mantua and the final round at Genoa, just edging out Guzzi's Balzarotti to take the title.

The second modified bike was ridden by Ruggeri and Bandirola in the junior championship events. But with the incessant development of the Saturno and the imminent introduction of Remor's brainchild, the distinguished career of the CNA-inspired water-cooled pre-war Gilera was to all intents and purposes over.

The outdated bike appeared sporadically over the next couple of years. Most notably, Pagani rode it in the Italian GP around the makeshift Milan street circuit in 1947, only to fall when in sixth place. In 1948 a bike participated without distinction in an Italian championship race at Monza and, with that, the water-cooled solo racers were finally put under wraps.

5 | The post-war four: to 1953

Remor's post-war air-cooled four-cylinder engine endured, with little revision, until 1953

The modified pre-war racer may have been patently inadequate, but immediately after the hostilities Remor was fully occupied in the prototype machine department. So it was not until 1947 that he could belatedly turn to the design of the long-overdue replacement for the antiquated, water-cooled 500 cc model. Working together with Giuseppe Gilera, he produced a bike which, with the benefit of constant revision, was to be in the forefront of racing for the next decade.

Remor's new transverse four-cylinder engine emerged as an amalgam of the features of the pre-war version and a 250 cc four-cylinder unit which he had designed in 1940. Like the old four, bore and stroke dimensions were 52 × 58 mm, and the two valves per cylinder were governed by twin cams which were in turn driven by a train of gears running between the pairs of cylinders. In common with the quarter-litre engine, the air-cooled cylinder block was inclined at only 30 degrees and a wet sump was incorporated. The separate cylinders were pear-shaped and four individual exhaust pipes were employed.

Supercharging having been banned by FIM decree, Gilera asked Weber to design a new 28 mm carburettor, one of which was fitted to each pair of cylinders. Magneto problems were solved by the adoption of a Marelli unit, mounted vertically behind the cylinder block. The four-speed gearbox was perhaps an indication of a fairly wide powerband or an anachronism, for Guzzi had introduced a five-speed box on the 1940 triple. A wet multi-plate clutch was used.

Faced with the customary Gilera refusal to reveal mechanical details, journalists were unable to prise information about engine internals out of the sphinx-like Remor. Whereas Carcano was ever ready to divulge the minutiae of Guzzi pistons and crankshafts whenever a new racer was launched, Fergus Anderson had to be content with the scanty knowledge that Remor had opted for coil valve springs on the basis that they were only a quarter of the weight of hairpin springs. Indeed, Anderson, who visited Arcore in his alternative role of *Motor Cycling* reporter early in 1948, was almost overjoyed to discover that the plugs were centrally disposed but masked off from the combustion chamber, with an oval passage running from the plug to the chamber.

This reticence undoubtedly did little to help dispel the oft-repeated, but nonetheless erroneous, tale that the primary transmission was taken, like the dohc drive, from the centre of the cylinders. In defence of the English journalists who repeated this inaccuracy with monotonous regularity, they had to surmount not only the language barrier but Gilera's obsessional secrecy over technical details. Indeed, Italian journals reported on occasion that the primary drive was taken from between cylinders three and four, and there was published at least one cutaway drawing to substantiate the claim, showing a toothed outer flywheel on the third cylinder. Franco Passoni, however, who was one of Remor's assistants in the prototype and racing departments from 1948, and ultimately his successor, confirms that drive was taken from between the first and second cylinders of the engines he worked on.

The only section of the frame which was reminiscent of Serafini's model was the central-spring, pressed-steel front forks. Although BMW had pioneered telescopics a decade earlier, many riders, both Italian and English, still regarded them with undisguised suspicion, as they tended to spring excessively under braking. The remainder of the new frame was nothing out of the ordinary and may well have been derived from Remor's ideas for the 250 cc model. A single top tube sprouted duplex front downtubes; the oval tubes, chosen for their rigidity and light weight, ran from the rear of the tank to the base of the engine-gearbox unit, whence they turned and ran forward to meet the front downtubes. An unusual feature was the rear springing; a pivoted pressed-steel rear fork, tapering from the front to the rear, was controlled by a spring plunger system, mounted behind the gearbox, with conventional friction damping employed. The large aluminium brakes were left-hand mounted in 20 in. wheels, with 3 in. and 3.25 in. tyres at the front and rear respectively.

Although the Italian multis were subsequently

labelled as cumbersome, unwieldy beasts, the 1948 Gilera weighed 275 lb which was lighter than a 500 cc Norton and little heavier than a 250 cc Guzzi. Fergus Anderson noted the extensive use of the latest materials and reported that the petrol tank was the lightest that he had ever picked up. Ironically, the red tank, which carried four gallons, was a bulbous inelegant affair, which no doubt contributed to the overall impression of the machine as a fearsome engine on to which cycle parts had been tacked almost as an afterthought, a necessary evil.

1948

The racer was unveiled to the public in the spring of 1948 for tests on the Milano–Bergamo *autostrada*, entrusted to the effervescent Carlo Bandirola. Bandirola was an engaging character, much given to riding under 17, a number generally regarded as unlucky by superstitious Italians. His colleague, the diminutive Massimo Masserini, was also promoted from the ranks of the Saturno riders to test the new model.

Masserini vehemently denies that the racer was a brute to handle: 'In its original form, it was relatively light and it was particularly easy to manage on a circuit such as Monza, where we conducted many hours of thorough testing. Our major problems were with the engine and Remor. The engine's response and power was unlike anything I had ever sampled before, but it was forever blowing up because we had a lubrication fault which Remor quite simply could not solve. He blamed the riders, of course. This lack of reliability was the start of the rift between Gilera and Remor.'

Masserini viewed Remor as something of a charlatan, largely because he felt that the celebrated designer had poached Gianini's well-established principles. Masserini also understood that Remor had unfettered access to Alfa Romeo's technical department and had raided their straight-eight design. The little rider bore no personal grudge against Remor, but did not share the popular view of him as an engineering Messiah: 'He was a theorist, not a practical engineer. For example, our lubrication problem was solved in the end by his assistant, Alessandro Colombo.'

By contrast, despite his personal disagreements with Remor, Taruffi regarded him as a demanding engineer who sought perfection, not as an argumentative tetchy academic. In the face of this gentlemanly defence, the hard evidence is that Remor was indeed a difficult so-and-so. This manifested itself when the new machine made its race début at a national event at Cesena on 9 May in the hands of the team's number one rider, the ex-Guzzi works star Nello Pagani. A disillusioned Pagani dropped out early in the proceedings, asserting that the machine was unridable, regardless of Masserini's confident assertions to the contrary. A sordid feud with an irate Remor ensued which regrettably deprived Pagani of a ride on the multi for the remainder of 1948 and indeed arguably cost him the world title in 1949.

Although undeniably fleet, the multi could not last the distance in Italian championship events in 1948 and the sought-after title went to Bertacchini aboard a rival Guzzi. The sweet taste of victory was, however, not long delayed. In July, Masserini took a four to his home town of Bergamo, where the Circuit of the Walls race was held over the narrow cobbled streets inside the medieval walls which enclose the idyllic hilltop city. Thanks largely to the generosity of his friend Bandirola, who considerately held back on the more manageable Saturno, Masserini took the bike's first chequered flag before his enthusiastic townsfolk.

Three weeks beforehand two of the new bikes had been taken to Assen, scene of the Dutch TT, for their international shakedown. Their appearance attracted one of the ambitious Japanese companies to the meeting, eager to shoot off numerous rolls of film covering the new

Gilera, representing the state of the art. Unfortunately, Bandirola's machine blew up in practice, but Masserini soon established a lead, marginally ahead of Artie Bell on a works Norton. With the onset of drizzle, Bell was able to edge ahead. An overambitious Masserini cast himself off twice in quick succession and was carted off to the local hospital. Bell completed a comfortable victory ahead of Pagani aboard his private Saturno.

The team forsook the following weekend's Belgian GP as it coincided with an international at Berne. Both Guzzi and Gilera enjoyed a hefty slice of the Swiss market and therefore plumped to race at the Bremgarten Forest track. The meeting sadly claimed the life of Guzzi's 'Black Devil', the 43-year-old Omobono Tenni, who crashed fatally in practice. Bandirola's was the

sole Gilera multi in evidence, but he suffered persistent ignition problems during both practice and the race, which was won by Lorenzetti.

In September, the Italian GP was held at Faenza over a particularly rapid three-mile triangular street circuit. The English teams chose not to make the journey, but nevertheless an 85,000-strong crowd turned up to witness the pair of Gilera fours challenge a trio of Guzzi wide-angle twins, one of which had been handed over to Fergus Anderson. (Evidently, Remor had been shrewd in not revealing his hand to the inquisitive part-time journalist.) The impetuous Bandirola led from the off, only to blow up without completing the first lap. Masserini assumed command and calmly reeled off the 50 laps to record the multi's first classic victory. He beat Lorenzetti's Guzzi single by over half a minute and inflicted further ignominy on the Mandello stable by lapping two of the much-vaunted twins.

The 1949 racer—note the eccentric rear suspension of Remor design

1949

When the world championship was introduced in 1949, popular opinion had it that the Arcore multi would be the machine to beat. Statistically, such an assertion appeared undeniable. The Gilera weighed 275 lb and the four-cylinder engine produced 48 bhp at 8500 rpm. The major challengers, the AJS and the Guzzi models, weighed in the region of 310 lb and their twin-cylinder engines were churning out some 45 bhp. The 'Porcupine' had been intended for use with a supercharger and inevitably faced carburation problems, while the Guzzi was essentially a 15-year-old design.

But Fergus Anderson, who was staunchly set against the concept of a world title, used his column inches to express his doubts concerning the Italian riders. The team's principal jockey, Pagani, still out of favour, was ludicrously consigned to riding his own Saturno in national events and the steady Masserini had hung up his leathers, having had to return to Bergamo to oversee the family business following the death of his mother. The spectacular Bandirola, albeit patently speedy, was notorious for his galling propensity to fall off. As back-up rider, Gilera selected the relatively inexperienced Arciso Artesiani, who had served his team apprenticeship aboard the Saturno.

The factory, as usual, shunned the Isle of Man, mindful of the costs involved, but, possibly even more pertinently, also through an appreciation that Italian riders would have little chance of competing on equal terms with their British counterparts over the demanding course. The dramatic Senior TT was won by Harold Daniell after Les Graham's last-gasp disappointment when his AJS's magneto shaft sheared a mere two miles from the finish. Hence, Gilera took up the challenge at the Swiss GP at the Bremgarten circuit. The race was dominated by the AJS duo of Ted Frend and Les Graham. Frend set the fastest lap of the day but then crashed, leaving his team-mate to win. Graham also picked up an extra, and ultimately crucial, championship point, which was awarded at that time in respect of the fastest lap, not of the race, but by a finisher. Artesiani came home a worthy if distant second, while the predictable Bandirola, true to form, crashed out of the race. Nello Pagani, who had been forced to enter his Saturno, such was the extent of his bitter feud with Remor, was fourth.

The next round at Assen was the scene of a convincing demonstration by the Gilera team. Pagani, finally restored to the four-cylinder machine which his talents so amply justified and demanded, toyed race-long with Les Graham, using full power only on the last lap to win as he pleased. Artesiani took a comfortable third place despite a lengthy pit stop.

Bill Doran won the Belgian GP, just ahead of the consistent Artesiani, who set the fastest lap on the final tour of Spa, failing to catch the victorious AJS by a whisker. Pagani limped home in fifth, having lost 600 rpm when a valve seat came loose.

The penultimate round was the Ulster, where a trap in front of the grandstand registered the following speeds: Gilera, 121 mph; Guzzi, 120 mph; AJS, 119 mph, and Norton, 116 mph. Les Graham won without ado to record his second series victory, which, together with one second place and two fastest laps, was sufficient to secure the world title, regardless of the result at Monza. Artesiani had been riding a safe second until a stone entered a carburettor, forcing him to join Bandirola on the list of retirements. Pagani fared a little better. He was hindered on the punishing seven-mile Clady straight, as its notorious bumps caused the rear mudguard to gouge into the tyre, despite which he collected third place.

Notwithstanding that the title was already beyond their grasp, the Gilera riders and team were, as ever, anxious to impress on their home track. Of the three machines wheeled out at Monza, one was equipped with discs covering

Remor (on the left) and Artesiani in the pits at Monza for the 1949 Italian GP

although both emerged unscathed.

The result sparked off a rumpus in the Italian motorcycling press. Graham had finished the season with 30 points, only one ahead of Pagani. A number of excitable journalists then raised the nice argument that the rule awarding a point in respect of 'the fastest lap by a finisher' should have been interpreted as meaning that the point was allocated for 'the fastest lap, if by a finisher'. Had this interpretation been correct, Graham would have been deprived of the point earned at Berne, where the fastest lap had been put up by Frend, who had retired. In the middle of the hullaballoo, Pagani was generous enough to acknowledge that had the rule been applied in this fashion, Graham would not have mixed it at Monza, because he could have ridden to a safe leaderboard position to assure himself of the title. Of course, the storm blew over, leaving Graham as the first winner of motorcycling's most prestigious title. Pagani did, however, salvage some consolation, as he rode to the 125 cc title on a Mondial.

At season's end, the irritable Remor abruptly left the Arcore stable. He certainly had a bit of a set-to with Giuseppe Gilera. This may have been prompted by the team's failure to clinch the sought-after manufacturers' title, which went to AJS. It was more likely, though, that the love of money was at the root of this particular disagreement. Remor had just designed a new lightweight production model and he may have been seeking a share of the profits—a proposal which his employer would not countenance. Gilera was not a greedy man; perhaps it was merely the final straw in their deteriorating relationship.

Remor now took his talents to the budding concern of the aristocratic Count Agusta in Gallarate. Over the close season he designed the first 500 cc MV racer, which emerged in the spring of 1950 with more than a passing resemblance to the Gilera four. Much to the chagrin of the staff at Arcore, Remor had

the rear-wheel spokes and Pagani duly rode this bike to victory, with Artesiani in runner-up spot. In company with Bandirola, they had led from the start, using their power to full advantage on the rapid circuit, but by dint of dynamic cornering Les Graham stuck with them, limpet-like. Almost inevitably, the exuberant Bandirola soon came down, bringing the Englishman to grief with him,

pocketed the drawings for the next stage in the development of their machine. Certainly, the MV boasted shaft drive and, at times, square engine dimensions at 54×54 mm, but in essence it was a Gilera clone. Remor also poached Artesiani, who was never to recapture the form he had displayed in 1949. Another more telling acquisition was that of Arturo Magni. Magni was a friend of Gilera's son Ferruccio; they shared an interest in model aircraft. However, Remor induced the young mechanic to leave Gilera for a new, and what was to be an illustrious, career with MV Agusta. So commenced a more or less permanent, occasionally acrimonious, rivalry between the two teams.

1950

Following Remor's departure, Gilera swallowed his pride and promptly re-engaged Piero Taruffi. The 'Silver Fox' was anxious to pursue his Grand Prix career with Ferrari and, subsequently, Mercedes and therefore restricted his duties to those of team manager. Giuseppe Gilera, a man who valued, and rewarded, loyalty in his employees, felt betrayed by Remor and was not prepared to engage another mercenary engineer who might pack up his bags and take the engine's jealously-guarded secrets to a rival team. He therefore promoted from within, elevating Remor's assistants, Sandro Colombo and Franco Passoni.

After a hectic couple of seasons, Colombo was to move on. His peripatetic career embraced spells with Bianchi, Ferrari and Marelli, but he remained on good terms with the staff at Arcore and later returned on a part-time basis as a consultant within the Piaggio conglomerate.

His junior colleague, Franco Passoni, had started work in the tool department in 1946 and had joined Remor in the race and prototype departments two years later. His father had worked for the company from its infancy and Gilera was confident that Passoni would not stab

him in the back.

The new design team was content to do no more than tinker with the bike for the forthcoming campaign. Passoni introduced two heads together with a full-width cam cover in place of the rigid monobloc head favoured by Remor, which the mechanics found excessively time-consuming to fettle. The carburettor size was increased to 30 mm and power rose to 52 bhp at 9000 rpm. Remor's eccentric rear suspension system was scrapped in favour of the pre-war arrangement, which had been retained throughout on the Saturno: cylindrical horizontal spring boxes under the saddle, with friction damping. A hub-width front brake was incorporated, but Passoni persevered with box-section front forks in the face of the prevailing fashion for telescopics. Gilera were not alone in this apparently perverse adherence to girder forks; both NSU and BMW, still outcasts from international competition, were experimenting with them on their blown models, raced in national events in Germany.

Artesiani's replacement was the slightly-built 24-year-old Umberto Masetti, who ran a Gilera agency with his father in Parma. Masetti had ridden a Saturno with distinction in 1949, quite apart from having won the Italian 125 cc title on a Morini. He produced a glimpse of things to come at the non-title Spanish GP, where he had led until clutch trouble set in on the last lap of the demanding Montjuich circuit. Pagani took another victory aboard his Saturno ahead of a gaggle of privateers.

As only the four highest points-scoring places out of the six rounds counted towards the world title, the team could afford to adopt its usual policy of sacrificing the Manx round. The Senior TT was dominated by the Norton works squad, led home by its refulgent star, Geoff Duke.

Gilera entered the fray at Spa, in a momentous Belgian GP, the scene of the début of the 500 cc MV in the hands of Artesiani. Bandirola assumed an early but precarious lead and then unwittingly

The 1950 version—following Remor's departure the rear springing reverted to the pre-war system

caused mayhem when he braked violently, thereby bringing down Les Graham and Artie Bell, whose injuries brought a premature end to his career. Duke soon eased through into an ever-extending lead until he was forced to retire, with completely bald tyres. The novice Masetti, timed at 135 mph on the punishing Masta straight, won from Pagani. Bandirola dropped to

fourth, while Artesiani managed a respectable fifth on the Gilera look-alike from Gallarate.

The three team members reproduced these positions in the Dutch TT. Once again, Duke suffered tread problems; this time he crashed out of the race. Pagani's challenge came unstuck when his refuelling stop was delayed by a faulty petrol cap. Three rounds had gone and the unknown from Parma led the title hunt.

The Swiss GP was transferred to the Geneva street circuit, which on race day was made treacherous by sudden showers. Pagani soon slid off into a barricade, but gamely remounted to

circulate at the rear of the pack. In these damp conditions, the Gilera multis were far from manageable; the flywheels were very light and engine speeds mounted rapidly, causing wheel slip. Masetti therefore rode with justifiable constraint and was unable to prevent Les Graham riding past to a famous victory, overcoming an excursion into the straw bales with his AJS. For once, the much maligned Bandirola stayed upright and recorded a commendable third place, ahead of Duke.

The penultimate round was held over the Clady circuit, which the Italian riders claimed was more akin to a motocross track. Duke resuscitated his dwindling title chances with an impressive victory. Pagani, who had been touring in sixth place, deliberately slowed on the last lap, surrendering the final leaderboard place and championship point to Masetti.

Duke was unstoppable at Monza and recorded a third series victory, but Masetti, who was collapsing with fatigue at the end of the race, clinched the title by riding to second place, finishing the season with 28 points, one more than his English rival. Alfredo Milani, who had been promoted from the sidecar team, rode a multi to fourth place, ahead of Bandirola in fifth.

The sceptics doubted the validity of Gilera's success, pointing out that tyre troubles had cost Duke dear at Spa and Assen and that the multi had been outsped by Norton and Guzzi singles on the fast Monza track. Nevertheless, the machine's reliability had been above reproach and Masetti had ridden consistently well. The young Italian was to prove an implausible champion; he candidly admitted that racing scared him and that he wanted to progress to four-wheeled sport. In fact, he was soon to test a Ferrari. He was also tempted to move to MV, but he opted to stay at Arcore when Les Graham

The 1950 squad, consisting of Pagani (no. 1), Carlo Bandirola sporting his customary no. 17, and champion-elect Masetti

Mechanic Fumagalli with the 1951 model, complete with telescopics, at Albi

went foreign, filling one of the vacancies at Gallarate. Bandirola did, however, forsake Arcore, taking his individual talents to MV.

1951

Giuseppe Gilera was too practical a man to rest on his laurels or wallow in the gloom of unaccustomed defeats. After each Monza GP, win or lose, he would throw a party for the team at Arcore, but within a few days he would review the lessons of the past season and begin to set down plans for the forthcoming compaign. Development work on the standard-bearing half-litre machine over the next three years was piecemeal, in part because the race shop was fully extended and partly because the bike was constantly one step ahead of its opponents.

In 1950, the Norton's handling had been patently superior, thanks to the McCandless-inspired Featherbed frame. Over the winter, Passoni duly took the hint and revised the cycle parts, using round tubes for the frame and adopting a pivoting fork rear suspension with

The GP début in Spain for the revised model in 1951— Pagani and Taruffi both look concerned

62

hydraulically-damped struts in the Norton mode. At the front end, the archaic girder forks were finally ditched in favour of telescopics. The tyres were fattened out to 3 × 19 in. (front) and 3.50 × 19 in. (rear).

Two of these updated machines were wheeled out for Masetti and Pagani at Montjuich Park for the inaugural GP, the Spanish, which had now been elevated to title status. Masetti rode to victory, but only after team-mate Alfredo Milani had been betrayed by his Saturno.

The Swiss round in Berne was, literally, a wash-out for the team. Masetti stubbed his toe in practice and was forbidden to start by the circuit doctors, both Milani and Pagani fell victim to the torrential rain, encountering steamed-up goggles and electrical problems, while Fergus Anderson splashed through the puddles to record a rare Guzzi 500 cc victory. The subsequent round, the Senior TT, went to Duke; again the Gilera riders were not entered.

After dithering for a few weeks, the team finally plumped for the new suspension system and all three models were thus equipped at Spa. Indeed, the bikes were noticeably sleeker; the cumbersome mudguards had been cut down to size, the bulky tank had been reshaped and a more businesslike saddle appeared. Additionally, a couple of bhp had been obtained by tinkering with the engine. A horizontal Lucas magneto was fitted, although a Marelli version later became available, and four Dell'Orto carburettors were in use; the sizes ranged from 25 mm to 28 mm, depending on the circuit. Although an additional 2 or 3 mph had been squeezed out of the machine, its weight was nudging the 300 lb mark.

Undaunted, Duke outpaced the pack of Gileras at the Belgian round and the next race at Assen. On both occasions he was followed home by Alfredo Milani, sampling the power of the multi. Pagani struggled to fifth spot at Spa, suffering from a misfire, and retired at the Dutch TT with gearbox problems. The defending champion slipped off the leaderboard in Belgium and retired in Holland, beset by the mysterious misfire bug.

Milani made no mistake on the super-fast Albi track, powering to his first championship victory. Only Doran on an AJS disturbed Gilera's celebrations, finishing clear of Pagani in third and Masetti in fourth.

The Ulster GP was tinged with tragedy, when the Guzzi teamsters, Geminiani and Leoni, were killed in unofficial practice, crashing head on, possibly because one of them forgot to ride on the left-hand side of the open road. Duke shrugged off Milani's challenge to collect his first 500 cc title, winning ahead of his team-mate Ken Kavanagh, Masetti and Milani.

At Monza, the Gilera racers sported a neat red fairing around the nose which merged neatly into the tank—a toe had been dipped into the murky and controversial waters of streamlining. Milani, Masetti and Pagani romped home to fill the rostrum. In keeping with his practice of encouraging promising youngsters, Gilera had assigned a multi to Libero Liberati, who, although he eventually finished seventh, had forced his way up to second place until he was thwarted by a broken throttle cable.

Alfredo Milani's runner-up spot in the championship was the talking point. The English press, and indeed the majority of the riders, hailed him as the greatest of the post-war Italian aces, a worthy heir to the tradition of Tenni and Serafini. Nevertheless, the undisputed contemporary number one was Duke. Taruffi recognized this truth and was not slow in trying to recruit the Lancastrian. Initially, Giuseppe Gilera, a patriotic man, was not over-keen on employing a foreigner. It was eventually his son-in-law, Guido Carnielli, who talked him round, arguing that only the best would do. In fact, Duke, riding the championship-winning machine, could afford to rebuff Taruffi's approaches and the glitter of the lire for a little while longer. Almost forgotten was Umberto Masetti, a man whose title seemed a never-to-be-repeated flash

Pagani's multi in the Montjuich Park paddock in 1951

in the pan, and who ran his personal affairs, in the words of one colleague, 'like a demented clown in a circus'. A lone voice, predictably that of Fergus Anderson, piped up for Masetti and, in 1952, he would be vindicted.

1952

The year 1952 was to see Gilera forsake his favoured policy of employing only Italian riders. In October 1951, the veteran French champion and Gilera agent Georges Monneret obtained one of the sought-after multis, which he took to an end-of-season victory at Montlhéry. He and his son, Pierre, were entrusted with two of the 1951 models for the new French season. Georges registered a fourth place in the non-title GP at Albi in July behind Jack Brett on a works AJS, while Pierre was to go on to greater deeds in subsequent seasons.

Passoni, heavily committed to the development of production bikes and hampered by a manpower shortage in the race shop, once again confined himself to minor modifications to the racer. The pistons, which were made of an aluminium, magnesium, copper and zinc alloy, had formerly been manufactured by Gilera; production was now farmed out to a specialist firm in a search for greater reliability. The nose fairing, tested at Monza in the GP, was retained, while a cowling under the engine was incorporated. The tank was also restyled, being shaped to suit the rider's arms and fitted with cushions on the side panels. With his customary eccentricity, Masetti sometimes persevered with the older version.

The season started auspiciously for Milani with the laurels at Faenza and Parma, but he came unstuck at Codogno. Milani managed to avoid a start-line incident caused by none other than MV's Carlo 'Bouncing Boy' Bandirola, but subsequently he fell off and damaged his thumb. This minor injury was to plague him and rob him of his best form over the following weeks.

Above **Pagani in full flight at Spa during the 1951 Belgian GP**

Right **The restyled 1952 racer with Masetti, Gilera and Pagani**

Jack Brett notched up an unaccustomed classic victory at the opening title round in Berne; all the Gileras fell by the wayside other than Pagani, who came fourth. The Arcore team opted out of the rigours of the Mountain course and Reg Armstrong scored a dramatic Senior TT victory over Les Graham.

Masetti and Duke, the major protagonists of the early years of the championship, fought an epic duel at Assen. The cagey Italian, confident that he had 5 mph in top speed in hand over his adversary, calmly waved to his pit crew as he started the last lap and duly pulled away to win by two seconds. Ray Amm and Milani joined in the fun in the fourth round at Spa. Sadly, at two-thirds distance, Milani decided he had had enough, as the pain from his injured thumb forced him to pull in. Masetti did just sufficient on the last lap to outdistance his Norton rivals. In subsequent years, Masetti has unfortunately been denigrated, classified as a 'lucky champion'. To right the record, it should be noted that a contemporary report stated that this performance entitled him to be regarded as a 'premier champion among champions'.

Two heavy crashes in Germany then effectively settled the fate of the world title. Duke fell in an international at Schotten and Milani

followed suit in practice for the GP at Solitude, breaking a collarbone; thus, the season ended prematurely for both of them.

Masetti was unable to capitalize immediately on his good fortune. He too was detuned by a practice crash at Solitude and, having fallen once more in the race, he limped home in ninth place, while Armstrong collected his second victory of the series. In the Ulster, Gilera's title aspirant was put out with clutch trouble. The team's new boy, Giuseppe Colnago, another of the Saturno brigade, turned in a game performance, snatching his machine from his mechanics when they were wheeling it away with piston-ring failure, although he finished well down. Cromie McCandless, who had been recruited on a one-off basis as Milani's replacement, came through the field to score a victory as popular as it was unexpected.

On to Monza, where Les Graham brought his development of the shaft-driven MV, complete with Earles forks, to glorious fulfilment, leaving Masetti (second), Pagani (third), Colnago (fifth) and Liberati (eighth) trailing hopelessly in his wake. The Gilera hierarchy, irked by this ignominy on their doorstep, lodged a protest and had the victorious MV measured. Domenico Agusta retaliated in kind, and the second- and third-place Gileras were wheeled before the scrutineers. Graham repeated the dose in Barcelona, but his final spurt was just too late in the day, for Umberto Masetti's second place secured him the title. In a gesture of goodwill, the publicity-seeking Taruffi once again engaged another local—this time the veteran Aranda, who came home in eighth place.

1953

Piero Taruffi was still embroiled in Grand Prix car racing, having signed for the Lancia concern for 1953. Nevertheless, he was simultaneously occupied with his duties at Arcore and determined to strengthen the team by signing Reg Armstrong and Dickie Dale.

Armstrong and Dale were introduced to the previous year's models at the Leinster 200s, coming home first and second. Armstrong, beset by gearbox problems, could fare no better than third behind the works Nortons at the North-West 200. Unhappily, the Irishman's Gilera kicked up a stone into Dale's goggles and he was rushed off to hospital with glass in his eye.

The team riders were monopolizing their early-season national championship races. Colnago was particularly impressive, taking victories at Syracuse and Faenza, although Masetti ultimately won the Italian title. Meanwhile, in France, Pierre Monneret was still campaigning a multi with vigour. Taruffi, however, was not yet satisfied with his cosmopolitan bunch of riders. Geoff Duke, following a difference of opinion with Norton, was spending his time testing Aston Martin cars when Taruffi finally obtained his expensive signature on a contract for the season.

Following tests at Monza in May, Passoni made a number of changes to the bike at Duke's suggestion. Although there were no significant modifications to the engine, the cycle parts were 'Nortonized' in an attempt to improve the wicked handling. The frame was lowered, the front forks were strengthened and shortened, the handlebars were removed in favour of clip-ons, the seat was lowered and endowed with a more substantial rest, and the footrests were set back a little. A single-pedal gear lever was adopted, as was a twin-leading-shoe front brake. Passoni had introduced exposed coil springs at the rear, but Duke preferred Girling units on his bike. A 4 × 17 in. rear wheel was also made available. Peculiarly, the machine shed its nose fairing and the sleek tank seen in 1952.

The TT was the season's first classic status event and Taruffi took eight machines to the Island for his three Mountain course specialists and Milani, who was making his début. In a record-breaking duel with Amm, Duke's race came to an abrupt end when he accelerated

Geoff Duke, Giuseppe Gilera and Alfredo Milani testing the so-called Nortonized model at Monza in 1953

away from Quarter Bridge, hit a patch of oozy tar and fell off. He was honest enough to admit that he had fallen victim to the fierce engine response, for the negligible flywheel inertia left no room for error. Armstrong was slowed with valve bounce and finally succumbed to chain problems. Dale was another to hit the tarmac, while Milani was never in the hunt. The Italian asserted that he was at ease over the demanding circuit, but confessed that he had not exerted himself unduly, primarily because he recognized Duke and Armstrong as course experts. Taruffi, on the other hand, recollects that Milani was less than enamoured with the seemingly interminable rain and fog, not to mention the early morning practice sessions. The manager was, however, delighted with the team's most recent acquisition: 'Despite his mastery of the course, Duke

Reg Armstrong lining up for TT practice in 1953

took practising very seriously. He would inspect the surface of the roads before and after a session and was quick to appreciate slight modifications to the frame or suspension.' Taruffi regarded the Englishman as virtually unbeatable and his view was to be borne out over the next few weeks.

At Assen, Duke was untouchable, while Armstrong (second) and Colnago (fourth) backed him up. Milani and Masetti both retired and Taruffi's problems then began. His career as team manager had encompassed many incidents which he had overcome with common sense and the advantage of his years of experience as a top-flight competitor. As a driver, he had often been frustrated by, and indeed blamed for,

mechanical failures and he noted that manufacturers were, understandably, not over-keen for their failures to be aired before the public. On the other hand, he also took note that drivers were prepared to attribute fault to their machines whenever possible. Therefore, as Gilera team manager, he fitted a tell-tale hand to the rev counter, in order to avoid 'misunderstandings'. He admitted that the move was unpopular with a number of riders who were prone to over-revving. These petty matters were as nothing to the dispute which blew up after Assen.

Umberto Masetti, as reigning world champion, was, understandably no doubt, irritated by Duke's arrival as a team-mate. His was a stereotyped Italian character—temperamental, excitable, mercurial. Outsped by his nemesis in practice, irked by the untenable situation, he packed his bags and returned to Italy. Fortunately for team harmony, the phlegmatic Milani was no

New recruit Dickie Dale prepares for a lap over the Mountain circuit

touchy star and was rediscovering his most glittering form.

Indeed, the next GP at Spa was to unfold as Milani's greatest race. Although Duke took an early lead, the Italian held on, and when the Englishman was sidelined with plug and piston problems, Milani rode on to a comfortable victory ahead of Amm. Milani recalls that day: 'The bike was ideally suited to the circuit. I could use its tremendous power to the full. In fact, Masetti's problem at that time was that he had lost form. It happened to all of us at some time,

but Masetti was unfortunate to lose his touch just as Duke joined the team.' Armstrong and Dale were third and sixth. The Belgian Leon Martin, who had acquired Masetti's machine for the day in another public relations exercise, was ninth.

Gileras dominated the French GP at Rouen with Duke, Armstrong and Milani climbing up to fill the rostrum. Duke's challenge in the Ulster GP was foiled by clutch problems, but he managed second place behind Norton's Kavanagh. Armstrong was fourth. Milani overcame an appalling start to master the newly-introduced Dundrod circuit and scythe through the pack, only to retire when in fifth place.

The leaderboard at the Swiss GP over the Bremgarten track was dominated by Duke, who led home colleagues Milani, Armstrong and Colnago. The team suffered a dual blow before the Italian GP, when Masetti withdrew his entry and, less predictably, Alfredo Milani pranged in private practice at Monza before official testing. Despite these setbacks, the first four places were once again the preserve of the Arcore factory riders; Duke, Dale, Liberati and Armstrong demolished the MV opposition which, in fairness, was only just emerging from the devastating blow of Les Graham's death in the Senior TT.

Duke, by now world champion, and Dale brought two machines to England and ran first and second at the Scarborough international, but their fortunes nose-dived at Silverstone, where Dale's engine seized and Duke tumbled, ruling himself out of the Spanish GP at Montjuich. In the final round of the championship, Fergus Anderson selected a 350 cc Guzzi with which he outrode the opposition in the rain. Armstrong challenged but overdid it, while Dale (third), Colnago (fourth) and Pagani (fifth) scored points.

For the second year in succession, Gilera had captured the manufacturers' title and, having secured the services of the world's finest rider, the machine was firmly established as the undisputed dominating force on the tracks. There was no shortage of rivals eager to tilt at the crown: Norton were developing their singles, with sophisticated streamlining options available; Guzzi were producing a potent in-line four; MV, despite the flight of Remor to the sanctuary of Motom, were regrouping. Mindful of the challenge, and of the fact that the life of the four designed by Remor was drawing to its conclusion, Gilera were now working on its replacement. The year 1954 was to see the appearance of an updated racer which, in all justice, should be regarded as Franco Passoni's creation.

6 | The Saturno

Following the acquisition of the CNA race shop, Gilera's former policy of racing modified production bikes was virtually redundant. The factory's 500 cc ohv models of the late 1930s, the 'four bolt' and its successor the 'eight bolt', were indeed raced with some modest success, culminating in Ettore Villa's outright victory in the Milano–Taranto trek of 1939. The 'eight bolt' was, however, soon to be superseded—its more illustrious replacement had already been set down. Designed by Giuseppe Salmaggi, the new model was to be called the Saturno, in keeping with the astronomical theme chosen for the

Nello Pagani riding a Sanremo model to second place at, appropriately, San Remo in 1948

factory's range; Mars, Sirius, Neptune and Uranus were other models in the Gilera galaxy during that period.

The Saturno was essentially a road-going sports machine, which spawned a number of variants, including the competition model which offered the refinements of a light-alloy head and barrel, bronze valve seats and an extra 10 mph in top speed. In truth, the machine was almost entirely lacking in novelty, the designer adhering to well-worn principles in choosing cycle parts: an open frame, girder front forks and the unique Gilera rear springing system perfected on the blown multi; 3 × 21 in. front and 3.25 × 20 in. rear tyres; a predictably bulbous tank in red, touched with gold. The vertical single-cylinder engine, measuring 84 × 90 mm for 499 cc, was similarly sparing of invention. It featured pushrod-operated valve gear with hairpin springs, valves set at 70 degrees, an integral four-speed box with a dry clutch, a wet sump containing $4\frac{1}{2}$ pints of oil, a Marelli magneto at the front and base of the cylinder, a 32 mm Dell'Orto carburettor, primary drive by gears and final by chain. The engine's purported 32 bhp at 5500 rpm propelled the 310 lb bulk to a top speed in the region of 100 mph. Workmanlike and unexciting the first Saturno might have been, but the competition version proved an instant success and its progeny inhabited the continental racetracks for nigh on 30 years.

Massimo Masserini, who had served his apprenticeship aboard the 'eight bolt' and Guzzi singles, was engaged to sort out the machine in 1940. He rode the prototype racer to victory at its début in the Targa Florio in Palermo and in the only other second category, or junior championship, race which was held in that truncated season, at Modena.

After the termination of hostilities in the peninsula, the tiny Masserini resumed his career and winning ways aboard the works Saturno in 1945 at Parma, Lugo, Bologna and Como. The factory's attention was nevertheless focused on

the pre-war racer that new-signing Pagani rode in 1946. This tactic proved to have been eminently misguided when the multi's days were numbered by the ban on supercharging. Meanwhile, production of the Remor-designed replacement was delayed by the perennial lack of cash and a consequent financial reconstruction of the company. Accordingly, over the winter of 1946–47, the Saturno was hastily overhauled for competition work in the international arena, as an interim measure.

The revised model was shod with blade girder forks, a hub-width front brake and pressed-steel frame elements, all unashamedly cribbed from the blown steed. A 35 mm carburettor was employed, weight was slashed to 265 lb, power rose to 36 bhp at 6000 rpm and top speed improved dramatically to a respectable 115 mph.

The 1947 season opened at the Circuit of the Walls in Bergamo. Masserini paraded the updated Saturno before his townsfolk but, embarrassingly, departed from the script by falling off and hurting his back. Three weeks later, at the Ospedaletti GP, Carlo Bandirola secured a handsome victory over the San Remo circuit, at which acceleration and handling were at a premium. Motociclismo subsequently dubbed the bike the 'Sanremo' and the tag stuck, describing the middle-generation Saturno in a most appropriate fashion. Bandirola was to repeat his performance there in 1948 and Masetti, Colnago and Valdinoci were to collect the prize over the following three years.

A few days after Bandirola's triumph, Jader Ruggeri notched up another victory at Lugo. Thus encouraged, the team resolved to embark on the reconstituted international trail. Impecunious as ever, Gilera tried to inveigle increased starting money out of the organizers of the Swiss GP. This unseemly bluff was called and the Italians duly backed down, sheepishly turning up at Berne. Unfortunately, Ruggeri was killed in a practice accident and the works Saturnos were immediately withdrawn as a mark of respect.

Privateer McAlpine aboard a Sanremo at Warminster in 1951

International participation was thereby delayed, but not permanently shelved, and Oscar Clemencigh upheld the marque's honour with second and sixth places in the Dutch and Belgian classics respectively. The Sanremo's finest hour was, however, to arrive at its home GP which, as the Monza parkland track was in a state of considerable disrepair, was held as a one-off over a street circuit in the centre of Milan. After

Bandirola and Clemencigh encountered setbacks, it was the squad's novice, Arciso Artesiani, newly promoted from the junior championship ranks, who inherited a distinctly fortunate victory, coming through on the last lap when Guzzi rider Balzarotti stepped off his Gambalungha, bringing down his colleague Lorenzetti on the Dondolino model.

The team's resources were directed towards development of the air-cooled four-cylinder model in 1948, but the Saturno was still in service as an adequate stop-gap. At Assen, as only one multi was raceworthy, a quartet of Saturno racers was available, some of which were equipped with Remor's eccentric rear suspension developed for the new multi. Pick of the bunch was Pagani in second place behind Artie Bell's works Norton.

By 1949 the multi was a proven winner, so the principal works team forsook the humble Saturno. The factory did, however, produce a small run each year, generally of between 10 and 20 bikes, for sale to privateers, through favoured agencies such as Masserini's in Bergamo, Merlo's in Turin and Angelo Grana's in Rome. The Sanremo's best performance in the world championship events was Pagani's fourth place in the Swiss GP astride his private model.

The modest Sanremo was still of use to the factory. Its competition department was divided into three self-sufficient sections, each with its separate budget, manager and team of mechanics. One was the off-road squad, which subsequently worked on a motocross version of the Saturno. The most prestigious was the Grand Prix race shop, responsible for the preparation of the standard-bearing multi-cylinder models. The third section tuned and maintained a number of Saturno racers, predominantly for the second-string works riders in domestic events.

The Saturno department at Arcore was under the nominal management of Luigi Gilera. Young mechanics such as Luigi Colombo would serve their time with him until they justified promotion to the elevated ranks of the Grand Prix spannermen. Giuseppe Gilera, ever eager to encourage Italian riders, would recruit them to earn their spurs on a works-tuned Sanremo, thereby meriting an opportunity aboard the glamorous multi. The Sanremo team's success story of 1949 was that of Orlando Valdinoci who, with victories at Forli and Lugo, captured the junior championship.

Nello Pagani enhanced the growing reputation of the Saturno in 1950, winning the non-championship Spanish GP around the tortuous Montjuich Park circuit. A promising youngster, Giuseppe Colnago notched up the machine's seemingly inevitable victory at San Remo, but regrettably this race claimed a Gilera victim. After Oscar Clemencigh wrapped up his bike in practice, the French rider Houel generously handed over his Sanremo for the event. Unfortunately, heavy rain made the roads treacherous on race day and the unlucky Clemencigh hit a wall and was killed.

There was little logical development of the Saturno which was generally left to the care of Luigi Gilera and his crew. An interim redesign took place over the winter of 1950–51 when Luigi cajoled Passoni's services out of his brother for a brief interlude. The sump was enlarged, the barrel's finning was extended and telescopic front forks were acquired.

Alfredo Milani emphasized the merits of the revised model with a stunning display in the first world-title round at Barcelona in 1951. He led straight from the start and after only seven of the 34 laps he had 16 seconds in hand over Masetti, who was of course on the multi. He recalls that race: 'I had built up a lead of about half a minute when valve trouble put me out. In truth, I did not need to ride too hard; the Saturno accelerated well, gave complete confidence when cornering and was perfectly suited to Montjuich, where our multi never really showed up to its best.'

Thereafter, Milani was promoted to ride the four-cylinder model in the classics, but the

Saturno fared nobly on national stages. The team's rawest recruit, Libero Liberati, enjoyed the spoils at his home-town track of Terni, Houel rode his bike to victories throughout France, while national championships fell to the Sanremo as far afield as Hungary and Venezuela.

The updating process was resumed and the third and final version of the Saturno emerged in 1952. The frame, although not substantially revised, was now entirely tubular; conventional telescopic springing appeared at the rear end; tyre sizes were reduced to 3 × 19 in. (front) and 3.25 × 19 in. (rear), and a 220 mm front brake was adopted together with a 185 mm rear brake—all these features were derived from the multi. Although the machine's weight was now 280 lb, the engine, with a compression ratio of 7:1, produced a healthy 38 bhp at 6000 rpm, good for 120 mph. The whole plot assumed a much more raceworthy appearance with a sleek tank and businesslike saddle, again culled from the four-cylinder model.

The new bike, called the 'telescopic' version, was given a victorious début by Liberati in a national championship race at Voghera in May. It was entrusted predominantly to the works back-up riders in 1952, but a production run was available for the following season. Thereafter, the machine swamped both the Italian senior and junior championships, although the factory's direct involvement was diminishing, primarily because the combination of Duke and the four-cylinder racer was proving to be invincible, regardless of the characteristics of the circuit.

The final embellishments to the Saturno were engrafted in 1955, when a dustbin fairing, akin to that of the multi, was made available and a 38 mm carburettor was provided, while power was boosted to 42 bhp at 6500 rpm.

The 'telescopic' Saturno, pictured here in 1954 guise

Although generally the factory no longer entered the model in international competition, its role was not quite played out. The 1956 Milano–Taranto, from which GP bikes had been excluded, was won by Carissoni aboard a works-tuned Saturno, albeit at a speed considerably slower than Bruno Francisci's winning speed in the previous year's event on a multi. This victory, in the last of the north-to-south cross-country marathons, was Gilera's fourth in the series.

Even in its last season of official competition, the factory was still turning out the Saturno and entered yet another representative, Giuseppe Cantoni, on a works bike in national events. He also competed in the Italian GP at Monza, finishing a distant tenth and, thanks to the bell fairing, managing 130 mph on the straights.

Following its withdrawal from official participation, the factory made a couple of bikes available, complete with refinements, for Liberati and Milani to race on a privateer basis until the hoped-for re-emergence of the multi. Predictably, both were overwhelmed by the full-blooded MV opposition, and in 1958 the old warrior Carlo Bandirola eventually secured the Italian title that his enthusiasm, if not his restraint, deserved.

Liberati did, however, give the Saturno one last fling. In 1961 he won championship rounds at Modena and Genoa in the absence of the Gallarate team and was only just pipped for the title by Ernesto Brambilla with his works 350 cc Bianchi twin. After Liberati's death in 1962, a number of much-modified Saturno racers were campaigned in Italy, most notably in the hands of veteran Paolo Campanelli, who had won a junior championship as far back as 1952 with a Saturno. The model still featured, although way down the leaderboard, in the Italian GPs of the mid-1960s and its competitive life endured until the close of the decade.

A little-known postscript to the Saturno's racing history is the story of the rarely-raced variant of the 'telescopic' model; this was the twin-cam bike, of which only two were built.

At the end of the 1950 season, it was a widely-held belief that Masetti had won the title by default, simply because the tyres on Duke's Norton had not been up to the job. This fuelled the conviction, beloved of Joe Craig, that the single-cylinder racer was inherently a better bet than a multi. Certainly, Carcano's Guzzi 350 cc models more than held their own against the march of the multis over the next few years; narrow, light, manageable, they were competitive even at high-speed Spa. This reasoning inexorably led to the conclusion that the dohc Saturno was built to provide an extra weapon in the factory's GP armoury. In fact, its origins were to be found primarily in Luigi Gilera's promptings.

Designer Franco Passoni explains: 'Luigi Gilera was running the Saturno race department, but he and the mechanics were increasingly frustrated because the bike was lagging behind the multi-cylindered opposition. He pestered his brother for a new machine which would give his team more of a chance, an incentive; it was as simple as that. Giuseppe Gilera regarded the 500 cc four-cylinder as the most important of his racers, but he relented to the extent that he agreed to release me to work on the new project for no more than six weeks.'

In the spring of 1951, Giuseppe Gilera uncharacteristically, and overoptimistically, revealed to Fergus Anderson that a twin-cam Saturno would be complete by June. Passoni eventually found the time to address the problem at season's end and promptly decided that as both hours and funds were limited commodities the existing Saturno frame would, almost as of necessity, be retained. He did, however, come up with a new vertical single-cylinder engine, but it was not until practice at the Italian GP at the tail-end of the 1952 season that the model was exposed to the public gaze, although it was not raced.

The cycle parts were simply those of the

The dohc Saturno engine designed by Franco Passoni

telescopic version, although the engine mountings differed slightly. Two faint touches served to distinguish it from the familiar production racer: the exhaust pipe, complete with megaphone, ran along the left-hand side of the machine and, in 1953, the rear wheel acquired a centrally-disposed brake.

The left-hand side of Passoni's motor resembled its precursor, with an egg-shaped cover for the primary drive. By contrast, the right-hand side had little in common with the Salmaggi-designed power-plant. The twin cams were governed by a Y-shaped gear train which was shrouded by the finning of the cylinder and the head. The crankcase had been cleaned up considerably; it now bore the Lucas magneto and incorporated the multi-plate dry clutch and the four-speed box. Predictably, details of engine internals were not disclosed, but bore and stroke dimensions were those of the pushrod model. Passoni designed a new built-up crankshaft and a 38 mm Dell'Orto carburettor was chosen. The machine weighed 280 lb and was propelled to a top speed of 125 mph by the engine's potent 45 bhp at 8000 rpm.

Both bikes were taken to Montjuich for the final round of the series at which Masetti hoped to clinch the title; the team appreciated the

The dohc Saturno racers both used standard frames off the 'telescopic' models

deficiencies of the multi on the tight parkland circuit and wanted to provide their star with another option. After inconclusive tests in the hands of Orlando Valdinoci and privateer Bill Petch, the twin-cam Saturnos were quietly wheeled away amidst a blaze of indifference and Masetti regained his crown aboard his supposedly evil-handling four-cylinder racer.

The dohc model belatedly made its race début in April 1953 at Parma. It was entrusted to Valdinoci, who led but was forced to retire. A couple of weeks later, he managed sixth place at Imola, far from outdistanced by the clutch of Gilera and MV fours which preceded him.

At the beginning of May, Nello Pagani retired in two races at Bordeaux and Aix-les-Bains,

troubled by ignition problems. However, the veteran Georges Monneret rode the second bike to the chequered flag at Bordeaux, registering the machine's solitary victory.

Masetti, Colnago and Liberati were others to sample the bikes, riding them in low-grade Italian events, without apparent evidence of exceptional performance. In September Duke tested a bike at Monza and became responsible for the only appearance of the machine in the British Isles. Manx GP competitor Harry Voice wrote to the world champion asking if he could assist his effort on the Island. To his delighted amazement, both bikes and a Gilera mechanic were offered to Voice, with the proviso that he should be careful as the team intended that Duke should ride the faster model in the imminent Scarborough international. So it was that a twin-cam Saturno raced over the Mountain circuit, but Voice was plagued by an oil leak which finally put him out of contention after he had completed the fifth lap in 15th place. In fact, the machine was destined never to grace a mainland track, as Duke raced the multi at Oliver's Mount.

With that, the brief and admittedly un-spectacular career of the dohc Saturno fizzled out. Quite simply, the dominance of the four-cylinder racer rendered Luigi Gilera's plaything superfluous, an unnecessary distraction. In 1958, the Italian press circulated rumours that the factory's racing department was preparing a twin-cam single-cylinder bike for a return to the

Right **Voice pulling out of Governor's Bridge in the Senior Manx GP of 1953**

Below **Voice's outing in the Manx was the twin-cam Saturno's sole British appearance**

tracks. Sadly, nothing could have been further from the truth. The factory's minutes record that, in the heartless manner associated with the Japanese mammoths in later years, instructions were given to destroy the first dohc Saturno in January 1958. The second model's appointment with the crusher came in November 1959. Fortunately, whether by accident or design, one of the two engines escaped its destiny and survives still.

7 | The glory years

1954

In the New Year, Alfredo Milani and Pagani participated in a three-race series at Interlagos to celebrate the 400th anniversary of the founding of Sao Paolo but were consistently outsped by Ray Amm on the latest factory Norton. Plainly, there was little room for unguarded complacency at Arcore. Franco Passoni had been

Ferruccio Gilera, Geoff Duke and Giuseppe Gilera—
pictured after a Monza triumph

planning a second-generation machine ever since Remor's precipitate departure and, over the winter of 1953–54, he undertook a timely and substantial revision of the four-cylinder model.

Passoni lavished considerable attention on the engine. Four separate barrels, heads in pairs, full-width camshaft covers—all were clamped to the crankcase by 12 long studs as before. But the 58 mm stroke was extended to 58.8 mm, increasing the capacity from 493 cc to 499.5 cc. The one-gallon sump acquired longitudinal finning and was elongated, which permitted the engine to be lowered by three inches yet allowed the exhaust pipes to be tucked in to prevent grounding. The valve angle was widened, growing from 80 degrees to 90 and eventually settling at 100 degrees; the exhaust valves had a diameter about 15 per cent less than the inlet valves.

Six main bearings supported the crankshaft. Gilera made their own one-piece crankshaft which was both inexpensive and reliable, with a life of between 50 and 100 hours. These commendable virtues rendered it eminently suitable for practising. For races, however, a built-up crankshaft, made by a specialist German firm, was used. A variety of cylinder walls was available; best results were achieved with cast-iron sleeves.

Primary drive was taken from between cylinders one and two, sometimes off the internal flywheel of the first cylinder and on occasion off a pinion on the crankshaft. The gearbox acquired a fifth speed to permit a bottom ratio low enough to eliminate any need to slip the clutch. Although Gilera experimented with a battery, it was decided that the Lucas rotating magnet magneto was more reliable; a Marelli unit was also to hand.

The cross-shaft operating the four throttles was carried on ball bearings, and each pair of flexibly-supported Dell'Orto carburettors was

inclined inwards, theoretically producing greater turbulence and also allowing the rider to squeeze his knees against a restyled tank.

The frame was not redesigned in essence but it was shortened, contributing to an overall reduction in height of three inches, while the pivoted rear fork was narrowed. The streamlined cowling, first tried in 1952, was given a fresh lease of life, running from the upper sides of the tank, around the nose and back under the rider's forearms with its padded rear ends forming knee rests.

Although he did not experiment with a 54×54 mm engine, as had been wrongly reported in the English press, Passoni extracted 64 bhp at 10,500 rpm out of the four cylinders. Against this, however, the machine's weight was inexorably creeping up; the introduction of a centrally-disposed, twin-leading-shoe front brake and the cowling, which was soon to grow into a fully-fledged dolphin-like affair, more than offset the use of lighter materials in the frame.

Pagani and Dale had been recruited, with impeccable predictability, by MV, but a string of clear-cut victories fell to the squad: Silverstone to Duke, Imola to a rejuvenated Masetti, plus the Leinster and North-West events to Armstrong. The last meeting disclosed a design defect in the valve gear, which stripped on Duke's machine; indeed, a recurrence of this problem beset the world champion at the French GP at Reims, where Armstrong faded from the reckoning with a misfire. Monneret therefore collected the first title round, with Milani in second.

The TT has long been bedevilled by controversial incidents, from Ghersi's disqualification in 1926 to the Crosby start-line rumpus in 1981. One such unmitigated fiasco occurred in the 1954 Senior event, which was delayed by, and eventually started in, typically foul Manx weather. Amm, seemingly oblivious to the atrocious conditions, rode like a demon and had a healthy lead when the race was perversely stopped after four laps. Perverse, because the

Armstrong's dolphin-faired fire-engine in the Leinster paddock in 1954

Duke wheeling out his multi for the 1954 Senior TT practice

weather was improving and those who had refuelled, such as Duke in second place, were inadvertently prejudiced compared to those who had run straight through, of whom Amm was one—shades of Phil Read and the notorious 1977 Formula 1 event. Reg Armstrong was placed fourth.

In a typical gesture, Giuseppe Gilera had drawn Duke aside before the start and ordered him to ride safely, forsaking the race if necessary.

Unable to agree suitable financial terms, always of paramount importance, Gilera gave the Ulster a miss, enabling Amm to notch up another victory. Thereafter, the 'Iron Duke' returned to winning ways aboard the dolphin-faired model at Spa and Assen. For the next round, the German, the machine was modified slightly; the streamlining was widened to cover more of the handlebars, while a 250 mm front brake was employed, instead of the previous 220 mm version which was, however, retained for slower circuits. In a dazzling race served before an estimated 500,000 souls lining the Solitude circuit, Duke just pipped the gallant Ray Amm.

A wet Bremgarten track, scene of the Swiss GP, seemed likely to favour the notionally agile Norton. Duke cannily lent credence to this sacrosanct theory by languishing behind Amm until the closing stages and then, in a convincing exhibition of the Gilera's newly-acquired manageability, he pulled past his demoralized Rhodesian rival.

Back-up rider Armstrong in Manxland in 1954

The fearsome power-plant, now revised by Passoni, pictured at the Isle of Man in 1954

At Monza, Taruffi, ever conscious of the nuances of streamlining, clothed the machines in an inelegant slab-sided dustbin fairing, although the pipes were left uncovered. Duke, topping 150 mph on Monza's straights, won with something to spare, while Masetti (second) and Armstrong (fifth) sandwiched Bandirola and Dale on the Agusta multis.

With Duke's championship sewn up, and the manufacturers' title suspended for the season,

Gilera did not attend the Spanish GP, which was won by Dale. Instead, Duke mopped up the internationals at Scarborough and Aintree while Masetti annexed the Italian title.

1955

Duke began the 1955 season with a triumphant tour of Australia, which had an amusing prelude. Tiny mechanic Giovanni Fumagalli sailed from Genoa with two bikes in his safe-keeping. Arriving at Fremantle, he was unable to converse

with the customs officials who, in either ignorance or generosity, valued the priceless machines at £20 each!

The bike now underwent merely minor revision. A scoop had been fitted to the front brake in 1954 to improve cooling, but excessive air pressure built up and so Passoni added an extractor.

A serious challenge to Duke's supremacy seemed imminent as Ray Amm had opted to go foreign, joining MV. Indeed, Umberto Masetti, tiring of his role as understudy at Arcore, had likewise transferred to the Gallarate cast. The first major confrontation of the campaign was at Imola. Duke stepped off, handing the Gold Cup to his budding rival Liberati, who was now

Armstrong riding to fourth place in the 1954 Senior TT

labouring under the eccentric misapprehension that he was Duke's equal. The event was marred by the death of the impetuous Amm, who came off his 350 cc fire-engine in his first race for the Agusta factory.

The title contest opened at Montjuich, where Armstrong employed his favoured tactic of increasing the pace near the end as the opposition faded. Duke led until slowed by a misfire, whereupon Carlo Bandirola assumed a handsome lead which Armstrong calmly reeled in to take the classic. The Irishman was a top-flight rider whose career embraced contracts with the MV, Norton and NSU factories. The solitary flaw in his racing make-up was his incessant and unproductive search for unattainable perfection. He was forever asking his mechanics to change tyres, brakes, engines and so on in the pursuit of improved practice times, instead of squeezing the best out of the model available. This characteristic led Taruffi's wife to dub him 'Armstrong the Undecided', a tag which stuck within the team.

A revised dustbin fairing was on offer for the second round at Reims; it was shorter and four inches narrower than those which Taruffi had

Duke en route to his runner-up position in the controversial Senior race of 1954

Team manager Taruffi, with Libero Liberati to his left, surrounded by race hardware in 1955

produced at Monza. The imperious Duke lapped all but Liberati and Armstrong on his route to victory.

After a warm-up at the North-West 200, Duke and Armstrong rode to first and second places at the TT, both on unfaired models. The race will be forever remembered for Duke's record lap at 99.97 mph. It was, of course, initially announced that Duke had cracked the elusive ton barrier, but the speed was corrected as the lap time was a paltry half-second proud.

The German GP at the stupendous Nürburgring was witness to an example of Duke's unrivalled professionalism. He had not raced

Duke perched on a dustbin-faired model for TT practice in 1955

there before, so he sampled 55 laps in a car to familiarize himself with the 15 tortuous miles of the scenic Eifel mountain course. The champion promptly broke the record on his second practice lap aboard the Gilera. BMW mounted a formidable challenge, engaging Zeller and Surtees on the twin-cylinder racers which, if underpowered, weighed a mere 275 lb. Despite losing 500 rpm because the fuel was of an unusually high quality, Duke fended off Zeller's bid comfortably enough.

Meanwhile, in Italy, Bruno Francisci was collecting his third stamina-sapping Milano–Taranto astride Duke's TT-winning machine which had not even been detuned for the long-

Armstrong in the paddock for the 1955 TT

distance epic. He left the Lombard capital with the rear wheel slightly misaligned, making high-speed handling unstable; the Gilera mechanics changed it at Rome, one of the six scheduled stops. Francisci averaged a record-breaking 78.9 mph, a stunning performance.

Left **The Monza paddock scene in 1955, with the dustbin Gilera racers plus Taruffi and Ferruccio Gilera visible in the foreground**

Below **Geoff Duke, pictured at Scarborough in 1955**

Resuming his title defence at Spa, Duke was thwarted by a broken valve spring. Nevertheless, Colnago (first), Monneret (second) and Martin (third) adequately maintained the team's stranglehold. Duke and Armstrong returned to their familiar positions on the podium at the Dutch TT. The event became notorious thanks to the infamous privateers' strike for improved starting money, which was supported by a bevy of works riders, with dire consequences. Gilera gave Dundrod a miss, but Duke confirmed his

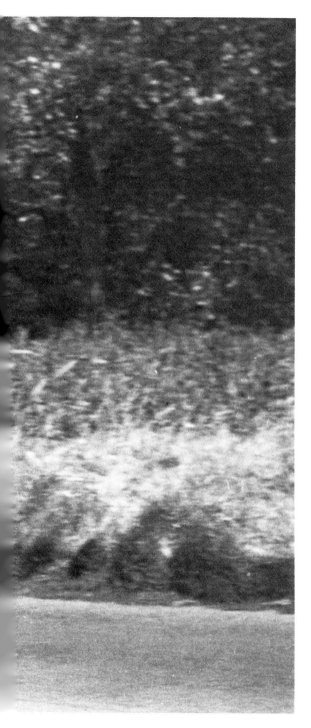

undisputed sway with victory at the non-title Swedish GP at Hedemora.

The team re-emerged in force at Monza, where Duke was well in command until his engine lost 1000 revs. The renegade Masetti, enjoying one of his all-too-rare inspired sorties aboard the MV, caught and passed him and won with both Armstrong and Duke clutching hopelessly at his coat-tails.

Eighteen broken valve springs had beset Duke and Armstrong throughout the season and indeed it was this epidemic that had blighted the former's chances at the Italian GP. The cause was the faulty heat treatment of a batch of springs. Regardless of this hiccup, Duke was champion yet again. He participated in the English internationals, winning at Scarborough and Aintree, but, astride a tired machine, he met unexpected reverses at Silverstone and Brands Hatch, where John Surtees served notice of his impending challenge. Indeed, Gilera were interested in acquiring his signature, but he opted, with foresight, for MV.

Such was the team's magisterial dominance that Taruffi felt himself superfluous; he retired as manager to concentrate on car racing, leaving the enthusiastic Ferruccio Gilera in charge of the shop. Gilera's nemesis was, however, at hand. For their bit part in the unseemly Assen fracas, Duke and Armstrong were banned from title events for the first half of 1956, while Colnago and Milani received suspensions of four months. Thus, the squad's title chances for the forthcoming season were savaged at a stroke by the heavy-handed FIM.

1956

Passoni, as ever, introduced a few modifications. The frame was revised substantially; the rear

'Armstrong the Undecided' at Oulton Park

subframe was strengthened by triangulation, duplex top tubes were adopted and front fork twisting was minimized by the use of a welded-in sheet-steel box. Passoni also designed a new dustbin fairing that was far more elegant than its predecessors, as an element of curvature was incorporated in order to reduce susceptibility to crosswinds. The exhaust pipes were furnished with megaphones and power was now up to 70 bhp at 11,000 rpm or so. The machine's bulk had grown proportionally—it now scaled an unhealthy 330 lb.

The controversial ban caused Gilera to miss the TT and its Dutch equivalent, at which Surtees ran up a couple of victories. At Spa, a determined Duke led comfortably aboard a machine which was recording a speed of almost 160 mph on the Masta straight. The gearbox ratios were particularly close for the race; the change from fourth to top at 10,000 rpm resulted in a loss of only 400 rpm, while bottom was too high for the famous La Source hairpin. With only two laps remaining, Duke retired with suspected valve gear trouble. Back at the factory, it was discovered that one piston had disappeared without trace. Presumably it had disintegrated and passed through the exhaust system; this was attributed to the unsuitable fuel on offer at Spa. To Gilera's consternation, Surtees inherited the race and thereby established an almost unassailable lead in the six-race series.

Surtees crashed and broke his arm in the 350 cc race in the German GP at Solitude, but Gilera were unable to convert his adversity to Duke's advantage, as magneto trouble brought his challenge to an untimely end in the 500 cc event, which Armstrong scooped. Duke's misfortunes persisted in the Ulster, where he hit the deck, and as Armstrong came to grief with gearbox problems, John Hartle scored a handsome victory.

The title had long since been surrendered to Surtees and MV, but Gilera entered an intimidating array at the concluding Monza round. Duke soon found himself behind Liberati, who had been allocated a more powerful and manageable bike in the hope of conjuring up a popular home victory. To the evident distress of the partisan crowd, Duke reeled in and then fought off the Italian pretender to record his first win of the series. With Pierre Monneret in third place and Armstrong in fourth, the Gilera team salvaged a little pride and prestige at the season's end.

While Duke wrapped up the Scarborough international with predestined inevitability, Reg Armstrong won the Avus event and thereupon announced his retirement. Monneret was another to bow out, to concentrate on his business ventures. They were replaced by Bob McIntyre, who had already rejected overtures from Guzzi, MV and indeed the Arcore stable for the 1956 season.

Sadly, with the tragic death of Ferruccio, Giuseppe's only son, in October, the fire went out of the team's belly; he had been the mainspring and was quite irreplaceable. Giuseppe's interest, not only in the sport but also in his factory's continued prosperity, faded and passed into a barely reversible decline.

1957

After the traditional winter tour, this time to South Africa, Duke returned to Arcore and sensed that complacency and inertia had set in. The use of dustbin fairings called for modifications to the frame, but his requests for the necessary amendments went unheeded. Riding at the prestigious Imola curtain-raiser he was one of a number of victims of the treacherous track surface, injuring his left shoulder. McIntyre, in dazzling form, was sidelined by electrical problems and Dickie Dale confirmed the newfound reliability of the exotic Guzzi V8 by winning the Gold Cup.

The almost universally loathed Hockenheim loop played host to the German GP. McIntyre's

Giovanni Fumagalli poses aboard a multi at Monza in 1956

early challenge was interrupted when one cylinder cut out. Officially, there were no team orders, but Liberati was undoubtedly the team's favoured rider and McIntyre was expected to toe the line. The Scot was in the sport to win and let it

be known that he intended to do so. Lap after lap, he pulverized the record, leaving it at 130 mph, until he ran out of time, finishing a whisker behind his team-mate.

In the middle of practice week, a brand-new machine arrived in the Isle of Man for McIntyre. It featured a lighter frame, with a detachable left-hand bottom tube which had originated on the 350 cc bike, and a neater dustbin, replete with

Last-minute recruit Australian Bob Brown prepares for Island practice aboard his Senior machine in 1957

pannier tanks. The Scot dominated the Golden Jubilee Senior TT, extended to eight laps. In a blistering performance, he turned in a first record-breaking lap at 99.99 mph, then broke the magic ton on his second tour and again on three further occasions, leaving the record at 101.12 mph. He slowed considerably in response to signals from Duke and Armstrong at Sulby on the last lap, but still beat Surtees on an unfaired MV by over two minutes.

Duke's replacement in the squad was the Australian Bob Brown, who had been a member of the circus for a couple of seasons. His aged Gilera suffered a misfire on the final lap, but he turned in an accomplished, if often under-estimated, performance to finish in third place.

The dynamic Mac came unstuck at Assen. Having stopped to change a rogue plug, he was pulling in Surtees when he fell; he may have blacked out because of the excessive heat. The unfortunate consequence was a neck injury which was to plague him for the remainder of the season. Liberati trailed home second, behind the reigning champion.

An indication that all was not in harmony within the Arcore camp emerged at the Belgian GP. When Liberati's bike would not fire up,

Roberto Persi, elevated to team manager after Ferruccio's death, commandeered Brown's model without a word of appreciation. Duke, at Spa as a spectator, was irate at this churlish behaviour and berated Persi, who would, like Luther, not recant. Liberati led the field home, only to be disqualified for having ridden his colleague's bike without notifying the jury.

McIntyre riding to victory in one of the greatest races of all time—the eight-lap Golden Jubilee Senior TT

Below **Brown taking his Gilera to third place in the Senior event in the 1957 TT series**

Bottom right **Duke, on his unfaired machine, riding to a famous victory in the 1955 Senior TT**

Libero Liberati riding to first place in the 1957 500 cc Italian GP at Monza

Victory thus went to Jack Brett (Norton) by default.

The penultimate and crucial title round was the Ulster. Liberati's success, as comfortable as it was unexpected, was ample evidence of his gifts over an acknowledged rider's circuit. In justice, Surtees had been riding away into the distance until his Agusta let him down, while McIntyre (second) and Duke (third) were still undeniably ring-rusty.

Liberati confirmed his title with a cherished success at Monza, while McIntyre languished in hospital, detuned after a bilious attack in the Junior event in which he had humbled the Italian. Duke (second) and Milani (third) concluded the team's season on a high note, with riders' and manufacturers' titles safely in the bag.

Even at the season's end, Passoni was experimenting on the machines with 1958's campaign in mind. Duplex front brakes, 220 mm versions, had been tested at Assen and some were used at Monza. They produced straighter steering, but the riders reported that too much effort was required. A new cylinder head was also under preparation for the forthcoming season.

Without a word of warning, after almost 50 years of competitive endeavour, Giuseppe Gilera now cried enough. Together with Mondial and Guzzi, Gilera announced their withdrawal from the tracks for three seasons, leaving the field clear for MV, Morini and Ducati. The ostensible reasons for this policy were twofold: rider safety and rising costs. It was certainly the case that the widespread injuries suffered at the Imola Gold Cup meeting gave cause for concern, and Giuseppe Gilera subsequently revealed that the factory's effort in 1957 had cost 200 million lire, an expenditure which could no longer be regarded as justifiable advertising. The overwhelming impression, however, is that these were merely cosmetic touches. The reality was that, following Ferruccio's untimely death, the racing effort lost its spark, Giuseppe Gilera his vitality.

It remained for Liberati and Milani to fulfil an obligation to compete in a short series in Argentina at the end of the year and, thereafter, the celebrated machines were returned to the workshop in Arcore for at least three years. A Golden Age, not only for Gilera but for road racing, had come to an abrupt end.

8 | The ultra-lightweights

125 cc

Soon after Taruffi's return to the fold, ambitious plans were hatched to compete in all five championship classes. Indeed, rumours were circulating over the winter of 1953–54 of Gilera's intended assault of the smallest capacity class, as it then was, but two years were to elapse before a 125 cc Gilera racer materialized.

Franco Passoni explains the lengthy delay: 'Quite apart from my experimental work with the production models, my time in the race shop was fully engaged, and it was not until 1952 that I

The 125 cc baby Gilera of 1956–57

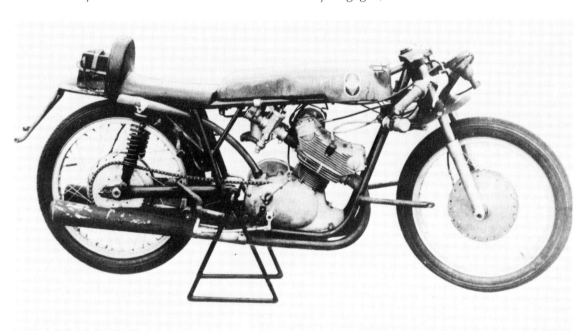

could turn my mind to a 125 cc bike. But then my designs lay untouched simply because we did not have the manpower to build the bike. Gilera would not risk the monopoly of the premier class and was not prepared to divert mechanics from the continuing redesign of the four-cylinder racer.' Once again, the lack of hard cash was making itself felt.

It was not until 1955 that Passoni was able to bring his ideas to fruition, encouraged by the heady enthusiasm of Ferruccio Gilera. Initially, one frame and two engines were built. The prototype exhibited few radical touches, other than the leading-link front forks, which were in any event a blatant crib from the class leader, the NSU single, as Passoni freely admitted. Surprisingly for a cautious designer, Passoni did, however, plump for twin cylinders, thus venturing into uncharted waters, for his was the first works 125 cc bike to be so equipped, although a private twin-cylinder Rumi had appeared in the French GP as early as 1952.

Although Passoni denied that he copied or was influenced by Remor's wartime design for an air-cooled 250 cc four-cylinder engine, it may be significant that he had been present at the final bench-testing of that ill-fated engine. However, he reasoned that a twin would have lighter valves, better cooling and more power than a single, so the step was both logical and obvious.

The team bureaucrats had determined on a blitz at the Italian GP in 1955 and frenzied activity enabled the ultra-lightweight machine to take its public bow at Monza in September, entrusted to Pierre Monneret. A handful of practice laps sufficed to establish that the new racer was too slow and it was whisked away for development over the winter.

For the 1956 campaign, a specialist lightweight rider was engaged, as Gilera poached Romolo Ferri from under the nose of the thrusting Mondial équipe. Ferri, despite extensive testing, was unable to come to terms with the characteristics of the leading-link forks; Passoni

duly ditched them in favour of telescopics, thereby slotting the final piece into the jigsaw.

In a sensational race début in May at Monza, Ferri led from flag to flag, trouncing the formidable array of talent mustered by MV— Ubbiali et al.—and rubbing salt deep into the Gallarate team's wounds by averaging over 96 mph for the race, more than 3 mph faster than Ubbiali's winning speed in the GP of the previous autumn. Boosted by this encouraging display, Gilera prepared four engines and two frames for the world championship events.

An outing at Faenza disclosed carburettor and gearbox problems and so the title bid was not launched until the Belgian GP at Spa. A record lap at 100.85 mph meant that the Gilerino was rarely off full lick and the punishing nature of the scenic Ardennes track soon took its toll of the engine, causing Ferri to relinquish his lead and retire. Monneret salvaged a respectable third place behind a brace of Agustas.

At Solitude, a fortnight later, Ferri had his revenge, winning the German GP. At the end of the first lap, the proverbial blanket would have covered Ferri, Ubbiali and Provini (Mondial). As Ferri tired of the dice, he simply upped the pace, collecting lap and race records as he registered the bike's first, and unexpectedly last, classic victory. In a dull processional race at Dundrod, Ferri was unable to mount the expected challenge to Ubbiali and lagged over a minute behind at the finish.

Finally, the teams returned to Monza. Gilera had recruited Enzo Vezzalini to back up Ferri, but he was an early faller. His team leader indulged in the inevitable record-breaking struggle with his MV and Mondial rivals until he toured in to retire with a holed piston. Ubbiali snatched a narrow victory from Provini. Although patently speedy, the little Gilera's lack of reliability had cost Ferri dear, even though he did finish the season as runner-up to Ubbiali in the title stakes. Ferri added an international victory at Kristianstad to his tally before the curtain fell on the programme.

Romolo Ferri taking the 125 cc bike to its solitary GP success, at Solitude in 1956

The baby Gilera had conventional cycle parts, featuring a simple duplex cradle tubular frame, a swinging rear fork and telescopic front forks braced by a welded-in sheet-steel box. Twin-leading-shoe brakes were employed, and the tyres were 2.50 × 18 in., both front and rear.

The 125 cc engine, inclined forwards at 30 degrees, was really a scaled-down version of the middle cylinders of the big Gilera, with bore and stroke reduced to 40 mm and 49.6 mm respectively. The two valves per cylinder, which sat at 80 degrees, were governed by a dohc assembly driven by the customary central gear train. Primary drive was by gears and final drive by chain, and the integral gearbox was a six-speeder. Twin 22 mm Dell'Orto carburettors, fed by a common float chamber situated between them, were employed. Ignition was by battery, placed behind the seat, and two coils on the front downtube.

One handicap to emerge during the early-season Italian events had been the product of the complete streamlining, which severely restricted the engine's air-cooling. Passoni therefore incorporated air vents in a revised dustbin fairing. This included a low screen section which extended back, necessitating cutaways for the handlebars. An extensive tail section was fitted, leaving barely sufficient space to accommodate the rider's legs.

Back-up rider Enzo Vezzalini on the grid with his beautifully faired Gilerino

The 125 cc model being prepared for the 1957 record-breaking sessions at Monza

The fairings were finished in the famed red and white livery. The slim tank, recessed for the rider's knees and decorated with a puny piece of foam to cushion his chin, was in traditional Gilera vivid red.

The engine, with a compression ratio of 11:1, produced about 20 bhp at 12,000 rpm, while weight, including fairings, was in the region of 210 lb, which permitted a top speed of almost 120 mph. By comparison, the single-cylinder MV had marginally less power and speed, but more than compensated for any deficiency in that department by a 20 lb weight advantage.

Sadly, the fortunes of the 125 cc model suffered two devastating blows, with Ferruccio's death being followed by a policy decision to concentrate development on a new 175 cc racer. The smallest bike in the Arcore stable was largely ignored and its sporadic appearances in 1957 were half-hearted affairs. At Syracuse, Provini aboard the up-dated Mondial, revised by Alfonso Drusiani and armed with seven speeds, out-paced Ferri (second) and Gilera's second-string Claudio Galliani (third) with contemptuous ease, a tale which was repeated at Ravenna.

Ferri was the sole rider of the machine at Hockenheim for the first GP of the new season, but engine trouble set in on the first lap. His entry for the TT was scrubbed and the machine's brief racing story came to an anticlimactic conclusion.

The tale did not terminate in this unsatisfactory fashion. In November, Ferri rode the racer at Monza in the record-breaking spree. The bike was enclosed in an all-enveloping torpedo-like streamlining designed by Passoni—the mechanics had to hold the projectile until Ferri, having clambered in, could put his feet through holes in the shell to keep himself upright. He then established the following class records: the standing-start kilometre in 28.5 seconds, at a speed of 78.5 mph; the 100 kilometres at 122.5 mph and the hour record at 123 miles. With that effort the twin was put under wraps with the fours and Ferri transferred his allegiance to Ducati to pilot the desmodromic 125 cc model.

There was a barely remembered and somewhat poignant postscript to the saga. In the mid-

Ferri is pushed off by his mechanics. The new fairing for the record-breaking attempts has not yet been painted red and white

1960s the factory, lurching from industrial stagnation to financial crisis, toyed with a series of bizarre schemes for a headline-grabbing return to the racetracks. One of the more hare-brained was that the ultra-lightweight machine should be resuscitated for Remo Venturi's use in 1966, a proposal which was properly met with short shrift.

Against this background, Scuderia Macar, a substantial private team, sweet-talked the factory into providing a couple of the machines for the 1967 domestic season, consisting of a paltry three races. One bike was wheeled out in June at Vallelunga, to be ridden by novice Giovanni Lombardi. The sleek all-embracing fairing had, of necessity, been replaced by a conventional dolphin, in white. The battery now sat atop the gearbox and a new saddle was featured—little up-dating indeed for a design which was into its second decade. The Gilerino was inexorably doomed before it turned a cobweb-laden wheel.

Lombardi creditably brought the bike home in third, beating a dozen privateers on Ducati machinery but trailing far behind Walter Villa on the latest Mondial, the nearest thing to a fully-fledged GP bike in the race.

The second round of the championship was held in July over the Zingonia track, a road circuit just outside Milan, named after Renzo Zingone, a wealthy industrialist. A second bike was entrusted to a celebrated name, Tullio Masserini, the son of Massimo. Tullio was a noted trials rider on Arcore hardware, but he had never before sampled road racing and he marked his début by falling off. Despite gearbox problems Lombardi fared a little better, finishing fifth.

The bikes, patently dated, did not participate in the final round and were returned to their resting place in Arcore. Thus, with Lombardi's unheralded fifth in the national standings, did the competitive career of the baby Gilera fizzle out, ignominiously, with barely a whimper.

175 cc

Although it was not a GP bike, mention should be made of the factory's last-ever racer. Perversely, just as enthusiasm was waning in the wake of Ferruccio's death, Passoni was instructed to design a 175 cc Formula 2 machine as a matter of urgency over the winter of 1956–57. These instructions were prompted more by harsh commercial reality than the factory's traditional sporting inclinations.

Giuseppe Gilera decided that, in an attempt to boost flagging sales, he would enter a team of young hopefuls such as Vezzalini and Galliani in the Giro d'Italia Motociclistico, a nine-day race over 1300 kilometres of open roads, based around Bologna, for sports production machines of up to 175 cc. The previous four editions of the Motogiro had attracted considerable public interest and success ensured substantial advertising potential which Gilera's rivals, and Ducati in particular, had not been slow to exploit.

Perhaps inevitably, the 175 cc twin-cylinder which crystallized just in time for the Motogiro was derived in large part from the 125 cc Grand Prix steed. Passoni confesses: 'If you look at the lines of the 175 cc engine, you will see that they follow very closely those of the ultra-lightweight motor. As usual, I was working unaided and had very little time in which to complete the task.'

The new frame differed in that it featured a single top tube and dispensed with two of the bracing tubes; the front and rear forks and the brakes were identical to those of its stable companion. The twin cylinders were unique for a Passoni design in that they were inclined forwards at only 20 degrees, but otherwise resembled the central cylinders of the 350 cc engine, having dimensions of 46 × 52.6 mm. Two 24 mm Dell'Orto carburettors were

Franco Passoni displays the record-breaking 175 cc engine to rider and journalist Roberto Patrignani in 1962

standard. The integral gearbox relied on five speeds; a 2.75 × 18 in. rear tyre was fitted; a bulbous 18-litre tank, in red and black, finished the model. Despite its 23 bhp at 11,200 rpm, the new machine's top speed was 10 mph down on its smaller sibling. Its unfaired state was doubtless a contributory factor.

Ten machines were readied for the Motogiro, which was destined to be the last of the Italian marathon classics before open-roads racing was consigned to the pages of history by the outcry following the Le Mans carnage in 1955 and the Mille Miglia disasters. The Gileras were humiliated, proving to be reliable but slow. The best of the pack, Pietro Carissoni, finished an undistinguished fifth. No doubt leaving a bitter taste in the Arcore mouth, the event fell to a 175 cc MV ridden by Venturi. Incidentally, Italy's perpetual runner-up, as Venturi was to become known, thereby achieved a notable and unique double, as he already had a Milano–Taranto success to his credit (on a 175 cc Mondial in 1954).

The bikes were subsequently made available for the Formula 2 championship, to the likes of Miele and Patrignani. Conspicuous success consistently eluded the racer, although Giancarlo Muscio did ride one to third place in the junior category championship.

In November, an engine was specially prepared and a frame adapted to take a teardrop-shaped streamlining for the Monza extravaganza. Two days after his 125 cc successes, Ferri set marks on the machine which established records for both the 175 cc and the 250 cc classes. The foremost of these were as follows: the standing-start kilometre in 27.29 seconds for a speed of 81.97 mph, the 100 kilometres at 129.39 mph, and 129.57 miles covered in one hour—all ample testimony to the efficacy of Passoni's streamlining.

Although one or two of the little machines competed in private hands over the next few years, that was the end of the factory's involvement with the 175 cc twin.

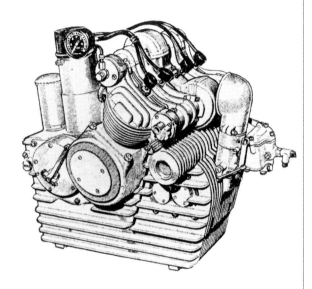

9 | The middleweights

250 cc

In 1939, Giuseppe Gilera foresaw that the blown 500 cc Rondine-derived racer was approaching the peak of its development and that its balmy days were inevitably numbered. He asked Taruffi to engage a first-class designer. Taruffi explains the request: 'I could dabble with a design, refine it and so on, but we now needed a really talented engineer to come up with another winner. I had no hesitation in recommending my former OPRA colleague, Remor.'

Remor's initial task, however, was to set down a bike for the factory's first venture into the competitive 250 cc category, which was bursting with works participation. In answer to the ear-shattering phenomenon that was Ewald Kluge's split-single DKW, both Guzzi and Benelli tacked blowers on to their outclassed singles. For 1940, the Pesaro concern also prepared a water-cooled four-cylinder dohc engine, armed with a Cozette blower.

In response, Remor was instructed to produce a similar Deek-beater. Plainly, the use of a supercharger was virtually mandatory and Remor adopted a central gear drive to the twin-cam assembly. These features apart, his new engine owed little to the CNA-based 500. The blower, probably a twin-rotor type, was built on to the front of the crankcase and the exhausts were thus rear-facing. Remor, like Carlo Guzzi with his new 500 cc triple, opted for air-cooling; he inclined the cylinder block at only 30 degrees and also employed a heavily finned wet sump;

A drawing of Remor's 1940 design for a supercharged, air-cooled 250 cc four-cylinder engine

Passoni displays Remor's pre-war quarter-litre engine,
still in the factory race shop in 1962

these were all features which were to reappear on the post-war 500 cc design.

A machine was not completed in time for the truncated 1940 season, but the engine was evidently bench-tested, as Taruffi was reported during the war as having claimed that 10,000 rpm had been extracted. Fortunately, the war left the Gilera factory untouched and the contents of the race shop emerged unscathed in 1945. The engine was brought out of its box of sawdust and testing recommenced with a view to racing in 1946. Indeed, an entry was made, probably optimistically, for a 250 cc runner for the Swiss GP at Geneva, run under the open formula permitting the use of superchargers. The entry, predictably in a year of scarcity of materials, was a non-starter. Remor almost certainly designed a frame, more than likely the precursor of his imminent 500 cc racer, but it is doubtful whether it was ever built, according to both Taruffi and Passoni.

In early 1947, Fergus Anderson, reporting on behalf of *Motor Cycling*, caught a glimpse of a new engine in the course of testing, but Remor refused to unveil its secrets. This was most likely the 250 cc motor, with its blower removed to comply with the new regulations. Franco Passoni recalls these tests and admits that, typically for an engine originally designed to run with a supercharger, they were not particularly encouraging. The engine was once again consigned to its box, this time for eternity.

Almost ten years elapsed before the factory once again considered producing a 250 cc engine. Ferruccio's insatiable desire to challenge in all four solo classes prompted Passoni to turn to the design of a quarter-litre engine in the summer of 1956.

Passoni conscientiously ignored Remor's design, but nevertheless plumped for four cylinders, in the days when single-cylinder models, from MV and NSU, ruled the roost. Passoni explains his choice: 'The deciding factor was that we had experienced such a great deal of trouble cooling the 125 cc twin when using a dustbin fairing. A four would have been easier to cool than a twin; it was as simple as that. Having made that decision, I intended to couple two 125 cc twins and follow the principles already laid down, with the engine inclined at 30 degrees and so on. The frame would have been identical to that of the big Gilera, although of course scaled down. As usual we did not inform the press, but the design was finished by September 1956.'

Orders were issued that the new bike was to be built after the Italian GP, but, before any work had started, Ferruccio died. The team's inspiration was thereby lost and the plans for the 250 cc racer were forgotten.

The chaotic assembly which served as the factory's racing department in the mid-1960s was a hotbed of more or less lunatic proposals. At the end of the fateful 1963 season, the factory, casting about for life-saving plots, contemplated building the discarded 250 cc machine. At this point, Passoni decided that the time had come to move on: 'I had been with the company for 20 years, but I could see that it was stumbling financially. I had a young family to think of and so Giuseppe Gilera agreed to let me go, on condition that I did not join any of his competitors.' This stipulation was a legacy of what Gilera still regarded as Remor's betrayal 14 years earlier—he was anxious that the other racing factories should be denied access to his secrets. And so Passoni moved on into computer work.

Passoni was replaced in the experimental and prototype department by Lino Tonti, another engineer without a formal engineering education. He had been involved in racing for many years with an assortment of machinery, including his Linto range and most recently the patently rapid but notoriously overweight Bianchi 350 cc twin, ridden with such gusto by McIntyre in 1961.

Derek Minter had once suggested that the old 175 cc twin should be bored out to 200 cc to enable him to campaign on the English short circuits and earn some much-needed publicity for the factory. His suggestion was given short shrift, yet, when Tonti appeared in Arcore, it was proposed that the model be entered in the more competitive 250 cc GP arena. Fortunately for Tonti's already wafer-thin reputation, this scheme was cast into oblivion. Thus, the factory never did compete in the 250 cc class.

350 cc

In the post-war years the relatively dowdy 350 cc scene had not been accorded overmuch significance by the Italian factories, which had been content to proffer distinctly unexciting machines. Even the current top dog, Carcano's fabled Guzzi single, was in origin a quarter-litre racer, upgraded on Fergus Anderson's recommendation. The MV Agusta concern also borrowed from an existing source, namely their 500 cc job. The Junior model that emerged was notably bulky and correspondingly unsuccessful. The lack-lustre class was therefore ripe for plucking and, in this stagnant atmosphere of vicarious design by adaptation, Passoni, on Ferruccio's insistent prompting, started to plan a 350 cc machine over the winter of 1954–55.

Passoni instantly rejected the facile option of a four-cylinder engine; he was perfectly aware of the inherent limitations involved in scaling down a 500. He reasoned that a single-cylinder power-plant would hand the Mandello équipe a head start and that a twin would be an underpowered compromise—this inexorably led him to choose a three-cylinder plot. Shunning the eccentric layout of the DKW, he opted for a transverse set-up, akin to that adopted so successfully by MV ten years later.

He recalls his design: 'The engine would have been much narrower than the four, and I planned a very light gearbox together with an entirely new frame. Ferruccio was all for it and I completed the design but, at the last minute, Giuseppe Gilera stepped in and cancelled the project.' In his customary cheese-paring manner, the proprietor decided that the business could ill-afford the new tooling and labour time required by the project. He was well aware that parts of the 500 cc model could be used to produce a competitive racer at a fraction of the price of the proposed triple. Thus, Passoni's ambition was held within bounds, not by the limits of his imagination, but by the financial restraints imposed by his cost-cutting master.

Nevertheless, the projected assault on the class did not lie dormant long. In an impressive burst of activity, the factory built two four-cylinder machines within a few weeks for the all-important Italian GP, which concluded the 1956 season. The engine was indeed nothing more than a direct crib from the existing larger four-cylinder model, with the bore and stroke reduced to 46 mm and 52.6 mm respectively for a capacity of 349.6 cc. It produced 47 bhp at 11,000 rpm. The size of the four Dell'Orto carburettors ranged from 22 mm to 25 mm, depending on the circuit. The frame was also akin to that of the 500 cc racer, but a detachable lower left tube was introduced to facilitate engine removal. The racer was finished off with a dustbin fairing, and a tail fairing, resembling that used on the 125 cc twin, was available. In all other details, to Passoni's acute regret, the machine was a replica of the 500 cc bike.

Top speed was a healthy 145 mph but weight was a penal 320 lb—only 10 mph and a meagre 10 lb down on the Senior version. Against this, the much-vaunted Guzzi may indeed have given away more than 10 bhp, but, scaling in the region of 240 lb, it could boast a formidable power-to-weight ratio.

The new Gilera was well suited to the Monza track and scored an overwhelming success at the GP. Duke's machine was soon out of contention with a rogue clutch, but Liberati, on its trouble-free companion, humbled the opposition. In a devastating exhibition of raw power, he savaged lap and race records and took the

The Flying Scot, lining up on the Glencrutchery Road for the Junior TT practice of 1957

flag over a minute ahead of Dickie Dale on the Guzzi single, now seemingly outmoded overnight.

The 1957 season, however, was not the unqualified success that this Monza performance seemed to foretell. By running the bike in the GP, the Gilera team had undeniably committed an elementary tactical error by showing their hand to the opposition, which was thereby given the opportunity to regroup over the forthcoming winter. Most notably, Guzzi produced a 350 cc

version of the legendary V8, but, more pertinently, Carcano made innumerable refinements to the single-cylinder steed, shedding about 25 lb, boosting power to 38 bhp at 8000 rpm and attaining a top speed of 140 mph.

The writing was on the wall at the national title events. Although Liberati notched victories at Syracuse and Imola, he was hounded by Guzzi's veteran Alano Montanari, who emphasized his point by collecting the intervening round at Ravenna.

The classics kicked off with the German GP at the uninspiring Hockenheimring. McIntyre dominated the proceedings until he hit a patch of oil and was sidelined. All the other works riders had, almost literally, fallen by the wayside, as the race was held in a torrential downpour, but Liberati remounted to take the chequered flag, ahead of Hartle's Norton.

A new bike was built for McIntyre's use in the Golden Jubilee Junior TT, with a lighter frame than the 1956 model which Bob Brown was to use. A slight modification to the engine was that the spark plugs entered the combustion chambers at an angle instead of being set vertically. On the Monday of raceweek, from a standing start, McIntyre demolished the lap time, slicing 41 seconds off the record to register 23 min. 14 sec. at a speed of 97.42 mph. Spice was added to the race when the Scot was forced to ride throughout the second lap with only three cylinders and, after a plug change, he found himself in third, behind Dale and Hartle. McIntyre would probably have gobbled them up, but his task was simplified immeasurably when a bird was inconsiderate enough to shatter Dale's

Bob Brown taking his 350 cc machine to third place in the Golden Jubilee Junior event

McIntyre, Fumagalli, Brown and mechanic Luigi Colombo in 1957 after Gilera's first Junior TT success

screen. The Gilera teamster was also the beneficiary of a patch of oil at Quarry Bends that brought down both the Guzzi rider and the Norton privateer, enabling McIntyre to romp home unchallenged for his first Tourist Trophy.

Despite shedding two megaphones and suffering from uneven carburation, the old machine rendered sterling service, bringing Bob Brown steadily up the leaderboard to finish third behind Campbell.

That epic TT performance represented the premature highlight of the model's brief career. From then on, the superior handling of the Guzzi came into its own. At Assen and Spa, Campbell unexpectedly beat McIntyre and Liberati, respectively. Despite suffering from severe headaches, the legacy of a tumble in the Senior event at Assen, the Scot returned to the fray at the

Alfredo Milani aboard the 350 cc bike with its special all-embracing streamlining for the Monza record-breaking spree in November 1957

Ulster. Having been left on the line with plug trouble, he had carved his way up to third place

when his engine soured. The team's other casualty, Duke, retired with suspension problems and Liberati was outridden once again by a rampant Campbell, whose Dundrod victory was sufficient to clinch the individual title.

The final round at Monza was not entirely

academic as the manufacturers' title was still up for grabs. When Campbell pranged in practice, Liberati became white-hot favourite in the eyes of the *tifosi*. McIntyre, however, was not content to play second fiddle; he wanted to race. The Scot soon displaced Liberati at the head of the pack and he duly proceeded to a comfortable victory, whereafter he was carted off to hospital, still suffering from the after-effects of his Assen mishap.

McIntyre and Liberati, tied on 22 points, were second and third in the title stakes and their combined efforts gave the factory the consolation of the manufacturers' title. With that, the official racing career of the 350 cc machine came to a close.

Mindful of the factory's traditions in the record-breaking arena, and no doubt of the attendant publicity, Giuseppe Gilera decreed that a full-blooded assault on a range of records would be mounted at Monza before the race shop was closed. The 350 cc and 500 cc models were prepared, with revised gearings, small brakes and strengthened frames. A special magnesium-alloy fairing was used, which had a sharper nose than the dustbin fitted to the racers and was extended around the handlebars. A streamlined tail was tested but rejected.

Alfredo Milani attacked and captured standing-start records on both models, which were good enough to take the 750 cc and 1000 cc class records. The prestigious record which the team cherished was the classic hour, once Taruffi's domain but now standing to the credit of Ray Amm. Milani clipped this by recording 134.4 miles, and he recalls his diabolical ride: 'It was extremely difficult because the track was very badly cratered and broken up. I was thrown all over the place for an hour.'

It has generally been reported by flag-waving British journalists that, dissatisfied by Milani's effort, Giuseppe Gilera ordered McIntyre to fly over from Glasgow to show the Italian second-raters how to do it. This is a transparent half-truth. Although recognizing and respecting McIntyre's unique talent, Gilera nourished a healthy patriotism. He had seen Milani, an outstanding rider, overcome injury and he had nurtured Liberati to the world title; he was not in the business of humiliating two top-notch, long-serving riders by needlessly summoning a foreigner. The whole truth was that both Liberati and Milani were already booked to compete in a series in Argentina and they flew off to honour this commitment in the middle of the record attempts. Alfredo was replaced on the sidecar by his brother Albino and on the solo by the Scot.

McIntyre opted to ride the 350 cc model on the basis that full power could be used throughout the hour. With standard Avon racing tyres and the twistgrip adjusted to minimize wrist strain, he had covered 54 laps of the parkland track when he coasted to a standstill, thinking that ignition problems had sabotaged his attempt. In fact, his unexpected speed had emptied the tank. Fortunately, the hour had already elapsed and the Scot had crammed in a sensational 141.37 miles.

His stunning performance had put the record out of range. The Guzzi factory, similarly proud of its record-breaking traditions, sent Montanari along to Monza with a 350 cc racer to challenge for the 'Hour'. A few laps sufficed to establish that an attempt would be doomed to failure. The Gilera mark endured until Mike Hailwood clipped it on a 500 cc MV at Daytona just before the USA GP in 1964.

Acknowledgement should also be made of Taruffi's return to record-breaking exploits. In the late 1940s, in association with his former CNA colleagues Gianini and Fonzi, he designed a tubular-space-framed twin-boomed car, which dispensed with a steering wheel in favour of a system of levers. He sat in the left-hand torpedo and the other boom carried a 500 cc V-twin Guzzi engine kindly provided by Mandello overlord Giorgio Parodi. The 'Silver Fox' drove

this unorthodox device, dubbed Tarf I, to six world records in 1948 and 1949, after which he turned his attentions to Tarf II, which sat the driver in the right-hand torpedo and relied on a potent 1720 cc Maserati engine.

In 1953 Taruffi, by then a director at Arcore, reverted to Tarf I and he naturally forsook the Guzzi power-plant in favour of a Gilera 500 cc four-cylinder job. On occasion, a one-off engine, bored out to 550 cc, was installed. So empowered, Taruffi broke another 18 records, including covering 200 kilometres of the Montlhéry track in an hour.

Taruffi crowned his legendary career with a long-awaited victory in the tragedy-laden 1957 Mille Miglia, whereupon he retired, thereby

Piero Taruffi at the controls of the Gilera-powered Tarf I

honouring a long-standing promise given to his wife. His final bow came at the end of the season when, with a 350 cc Gilera multi installed in Tarf I, he collected seven more class records at Monza. The last of these was the standing-start kilometre, achieved at night in the bright glare of floodlights and recorded for posterity by the cameras of Italian television. So it was that over 20 years of fruitful co-operation between Taruffi and Gilera concluded in a blaze of publicity and success.

10 | Sidecars

Unique amongst the Italian factories, which have traditionally shunned the sidecar category as an eccentric irrelevance, Gilera competed, enthusiastically if erratically, in the class from the mid-1920s until 1964. For the majority of these years, the leading light was Luigi Gilera, 'Luisin', initially as exponent and subsequently as mentor

Luigi Gilera photographed in the 1920s on one of the modest sidecar racers of that era

to the likes of world championship runners-up Ercole Frigerio and Albino Milani.

The earliest success recorded by Gilera outfits occurred in 1928, when a trio consisting of Luigi, Rosolino Grana and Angelo Fumagalli, riding 350 cc sv models, captured the team prize in the Trophy of 1000 Kilometres. Over the next decade, quite apart from his contribution to the 1930 and 1931 ISDT triumphs, Luigi Gilera regularly chalked up victories on the 500 cc sv three-wheeler over local courses such as Bergamo (1929), Como–Brunate (1930) and Verona (1935). Valentino Grana took the laurels at the Circuit of Bergamo in 1934 and Felice Macchi did likewise at Verona three years later. The major sidecar prize collected by the Gilera stable during these years went to the faithful Rosolino Grana, who won the Milano–Taranto marathon in 1935 at 47.91 mph. Interestingly, the chairs were left-hand mounted.

These were essentially amateur homespun efforts on production models, but Luigi was to be thrust into the limelight with the onset of the blown four-cylinder racing engine. He entered a sidecar for the Swiss GP in 1937, but was unable to coax an engine out of Taruffi because it was still at the experimental stage. In 1938, Luigi was more successful and he commandeered one of the previous year's tubular-framed solo models. He dispensed with the rear suspension and tacked a touring chair on to the left-hand side. Top speed of the projectile was 112 mph. Predictably, he decimated the motley assembly which made up the sidecar field of the Milano–Taranto epic, blasting to victory at the record speed of 51.13 mph. He repeated the dominating performance in 1939, but was denied a hat trick in the following year when he was forced to retire, having led for most of the strenuous trek. Some consolation for the team was that Felice Macchi led home the three-wheeler class astride a single-cylinder model.

Perversely, although Luigi Gilera invariably travelled around the Continent with the solo team, he did not enter his fearsome four-cylinder outfit in the classic events. Indeed, he usually confined himself to single-cylinder power in Italian races, winning at Pavia and Taranto in 1938. A couple of victories on the single at Voghera and Arona in 1946, and fourth place in the Swiss GP on the multi, concluded Luigi's competitive career.

The Gilera teamsters who were to be groomed for the imminent world title series consisted of a new generation of sidecar racers. Undoubtedly the pick of the bunch was Ercole Frigerio, from Treviglio, near Bergamo, who worked in the experimental department at Arcore and was the recipient of the most potent sidecar machinery the factory could provide. He was supported by Ernesto Merlo, who ran a Gilera agency in Turin together with his father Clemente, who, riding a SIAMT, had beaten Giuseppe Gilera at *La Gazzetta dello Sport*'s Festival meeting in far-off 1912. Back-up came in the form of the Milani brothers, Albino and Alfredo, who, together with a third brother Rossano, were also to become Gilera agents in Milan.

In the immediate post-war years, combinations were nothing more sophisticated than solos with a rudimentary platform bolted on. Then, as ever since, the unfashionable class was the preserve of the inventive engineer-cum-rider rather than the publicity-seeking factories. Design was in its infancy, although Guzzi did produce a hinged outfit for Luigi Cavanna, with the notional chairman positioned astride the pillion—a device of dubious legality. Throughout 1946 and 1947, the Italian and Swiss national events were cleaned up by the Saturno-engined outfits and, consequently, the Gilera charioteers were denied a run with the precious new multi.

The Saturno models began to encounter some stiff Norton-engined opposition in 1948. In-

Luigi Gilera riding to fourth place in the 1946 Swiss GP on the supercharged four-cylinder pre-war outfit

dicative of the state of play was the Belgian GP at Spa. Frans Vanderschrick, Eric Oliver and Hans Haldemann occupied the podium, while Alfredo Milani trailed home in fourth. Brother Albino was reported by the press as having looped, which was not the whole truth. By then Oliver had been joined by tiro-journalist Denis Jenkinson, who explains the proceedings: 'Alfredo was a neat, impressive rider and a good sport; he could accept that Eric could outride him. Albino on the other hand could be a dirty so-and-so and would not always play fair. As we overtook him he deliberately forced us on to the grass. Eric was a clean rider until he was crossed, and on this occasion he retaliated by intentionally pushing Albino off at the next corner, although I did not realize what had happened until he explained at the end of the race.'

When the world championship system was introduced in 1949, the sidecar category had a 600 cc upper limit. Alone among the factories, Gilera determined to launch an assault on the three-race series with Saturno-engined models, stretched to 84×105 mm for 582 cc.

The first event, the Swiss GP, was held at the Bremgarten Forest circuit. Oliver and Jenkinson dominated, leading from flag to flag, well ahead of Frigerio and Haldemann. Their performance, which incorporated a hastily improvised refuelling pit stop, so impressed the watching Joe Craig that thereafter he proffered special works bits and pieces.

The second round at Spa was the scene of an equally impressive endeavour. Oliver and Jenkinson suffered a leak from the carburettor, which the passenger stemmed with his thumb, precluding acrobatics on the left-hand turns. Despite this setback, they staved off Vanderschrick's Norton and Merlo on the solitary surviving Gilera.

The two incident-laden victories secured Oliver and his chairman the title and the latter explains the background: 'Almost uniquely, we applied science to the sport; for example, we constantly practised three-stride starting to ensure that we were never headed; we used purpose-built outfits and I applied thought to my job. Whereas the Italians passengered by guts alone, Bob Clements (Cyril Smith's passenger) and I thought about the distribution of weight when cornering and minimizing frontal area. The Italians were all over the show, with their legs in the airstream; hopeless!'

Although the title was already in the bag, Oliver journeyed to Monza for the final round. He had the option of racing at Lausanne for greater prize money, but he savoured the challenge of dicing with Frigerio, whom he regarded as 'racing with his head'. Gilera countered by wheeling out the old water-cooled four-cylinder model for Frigerio. Shorn of its blower, replaced by two carburettors, the engine was in the form raced by Pagani in Italy in 1946. Having led initially, Oliver suffered notional plug trouble and finally finished fifth. In fact, Oliver, inserting a hard plug just before the start, had pulled the spanner down on to the head, mistakenly thinking that the plug was tight; inevitably, it soon blew out. Thus Frigerio and passenger Ezio Ricotti rode to an unchallenged victory on the veteran multi and thereby clinched runner-up spot in the championship stakes.

Mention should be made of the unique machine ridden to sixth place by Jakob Keller. Keller was a Swiss garage owner, an engineer rather than a racer, who had been designing eccentric sidecar specials for a good many years. His latest creation was powered by a modified Saturno, which boasted a dohc head, driven by a Y-shaped gear train running up the right-hand side of the engine. The outfit was entered as 'Eigenbau' and gave Keller a run of respectable leaderboard placings in the early years of the title series.

The early months of 1950 augured well for the Gilera squad. The title-winning partnership was dissolved when Oliver was injured and Jenkinson teamed up with the Belgian BMW rider Masuy. At

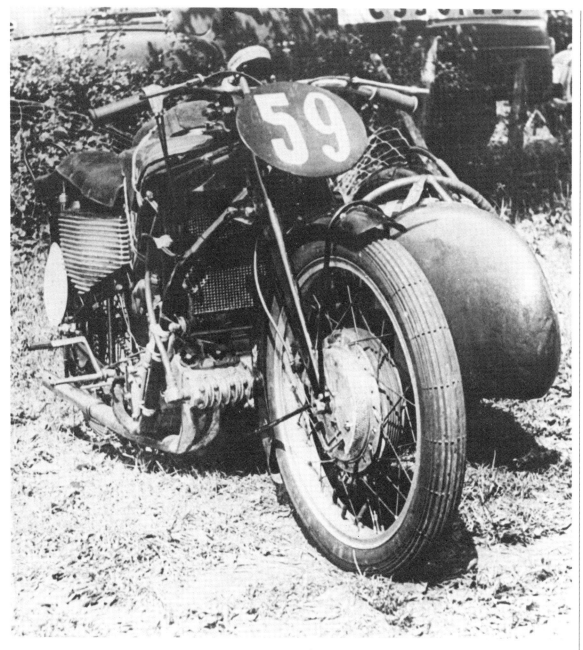

The pre-war multi, shorn of its blower, as used by
Ercole Frigerio at the Belgian GP of 1950

Montjuich Park, Alfredo Milani on the Saturno-engined model took advantage of Oliver's enforced absence to win the non-championship Spanish GP. Luigi Marcelli, on a similar machine, won the Milano–Taranto sidecar category, a success that he was to repeat in 1951.

When the classics arrived, it was a different story. Oliver, who after a period of flux with ballastmen was to commandeer Marcelli's passenger Lorenzo Dobelli, won the rounds at Spa and Geneva. Frigerio had raced the old multi in the Belgian GP, but had been awarded a new air-cooled four-cylinder engine, which was inserted in a rigid frame, for the Swiss round. It was to no avail; he finished 40 seconds behind the maestro.

The final round was at Monza once again and Gilera certainly conjured up some speed for their ace. Indeed, it was rumoured that Frigerio's air-cooled engine had been bored out to 600 cc; this was improbable, but practice satisfied Oliver that his Norton was 8 mph down on the multi in top speed. The champion's third victory was largely attributable to his tactical genius. He took to braking early on one of the turns after Lesmo, allowing Frigerio to pass him. On the last lap, the wily Oliver braked at the last minute as he entered this bend, barely scraping round. Taken by surprise, Frigerio tried to emulate the master but instead ran wide, striking the straw bales. He recovered to take second place in both the race and the championship. Behind Haldemann in a distant third, Keller brought his unorthodox Saturno home fourth, while Ernesto Merlo gave a final outing to the water-cooled multi, which took a farewell fifth place before being pensioned off.

The capacity limit was lowered to 500 cc for 1951, which was very much a repeat story, as

Albino Milani taking the air-cooled multi to victory in the 1952 Swiss GP at Berne

Milani and passenger Pizzocri, duly garlanded at Berne in 1952

Gilera and Norton were the only factories to display any interest in the class. The season started predictably at the Spanish GP over the parkland circuit in Barcelona; Oliver first, Frigerio in second on the four-cylinder, and Albino Milani in third with Saturno power.

Frigerio and regular passenger Ricotti managed to notch a win, albeit by default, at Berne. With one lap remaining, Oliver's primary chain broke and he had to be content with an unaccustomed fifth place, behind Milani and Merlo on Saturno-engined models. A trouble-free run at Spa redressed the balance as Oliver took the expected victory ahead of his Gilera rivals.

The fourth race of the extended series was held at the $5\frac{1}{2}$-mile Raymond Sommer circuit in Albi. The sidecar race was memorable for another exhibition of Oliver's tactical awareness. The championship had reached a delicate stage: Frigerio's 20 points against Oliver's 18. The Italian was determined not to be beaten and was braking very late in practice, which did not pass unnoticed by the champion. On the first lap of the race, Oliver allowed himself to be outbraked by his rival at every corner until he came to a sharp right-hander at which he braked at the last split-second. The crafty Englishman's ploy worked to perfection. Frigerio, intent on outdoing his rival, indeed braked later, thereby casting the plot up the slip road, kindly provided by Oliver's forethought. The Italian recovered, but he could fare no better than second behind the untouchable title-holder.

Thus far, Gilera had not transplanted their modifications from the solo to Frigerio's sidecar, which essentially remained a solo with a platform bolted on almost as an afterthought. Earlier in 1951, the solo racers had adopted telescopic front forks, but it was not until the Monza round that Frigerio dispensed with girders and took on a swinging-arm back end and telescopics at the front which were reinforced by a massive U-shaped brace. Sadly for the spectacle, Frigerio went out on the first lap, but Gilera had given a second multi to Albino Milani. By dint of enthusiastic cornering, Oliver kept pace with the Italian outfit, but on the finishing straight its acceleration carried Milani to a narrow victory. Oliver, however, maintained his monopoly of the title, with Frigerio once again in second spot.

The 1952 season began atrociously for the team from Arcore. At the opening GP at Berne,

Oliver was *hors de combat* with a broken leg, enabling Albino Milani and passenger Giuseppe Pizzocri to cruise to victory ahead of Cyril Smith on his standard Norton. After a sluggish start, Ercole Frigerio gradually climbed through the pack, setting the fastest lap in the process, only to swerve on the Tenni curve and be thrown against the trees lining the circuit. He was killed instantly. Passenger Ricotti suffered a broken leg.

For the new campaign, Passoni and Taruffi had made a serious effort to update the four-cylinder machines, which retained the elementary nose fairing, telescopics and brace, and now sported sidecar wheel suspension. Following Frigerio's death, the second multi was entrusted to Merlo, as Alfredo Milani was now firmly enthroned on the solo. At Spa, Oliver overcame his injuries to outride Milani, winning by 100th of a second. Smith, now armed with a factory engine, was third ahead of Merlo. Both Gilera outfits had dispensed with the sidecar suspension.

At the Solitude circuit for round three, an overexuberant Milani looped and was carted off to hospital with a damaged shoulder. Oliver's sidecar axle broke on the penultimate lap, leaving the remaining two works riders scrapping until the last corner. Cyril Smith snatched the verdict from Merlo on the line, but the margin was wafer-thin.

Merlo put his superior power to full use at the Italian GP, by starting so rapidly that neither Oliver nor Smith could obtain the necessary tow. Merlo simply disappeared into the distance for his first championship victory, ahead of Smith and a still-detuned Milani.

With one round remaining, the points table stood at Smith with 24, Milani with 18 and Merlo with 17. Milani, suffering from his injuries incurred at Solitude, was ruled out of the Montjuich decider. Merlo had to win and hope that Smith failed. Norton allocated a new works engine to Oliver and Gilera countered, rather more in hope than expectation, by assigning the back-up multi to Keller. Although Smith's frame

snapped on the first lap, he soldiered on to take third place. His championship success was in any event guaranteed by Oliver's comfortable win. Merlo, despite a fiery fastest lap, retired with ignition failure. Keller was completely unable to come to terms with the savage engine and quietly disappeared.

There were rumours that Oliver and Haldemann were offered mouth-watering contracts, which they rejected, preferring to outride the Italian machines than to take them to unhindered victory. Much to the disappointment of the Italian riders, Gilera then withdrew from the sidecar class, opting to concentrate on the 500 cc category and, ever a pertinent consideration, save lire.

This self-imposed withdrawal lasted for two complete seasons, 1953 and 1954, during which Milani and Merlo campaigned private Saturno-engined combinations in Italian events and the occasional classic round. Indeed, these machines virtually monopolized the Italian championship, taking five titles in six years, with Frigerio (1949 and 1950), Albino Milani (1951) and Merlo (1952 and 1954).

Gilera's exile concluded in 1955, but there had been considerable development in the intervening years. Outfits had become sleeker and lower, with smaller sidecar wheels and fuller fairings. The horizontally opposed BMW twin-cylinder engine had emerged as the power-plant to beat, thanks to its low centre of gravity and the support of the Bavarian factory.

In 1955 Ferruccio was approached by Jakob Keller with a tempting proposal. The regulations for some classic meetings stated that only sidecars could be entered, whereas Italian GP regulations permitted a three-wheeler to participate. Keller suggested that he should build a trike to be powered by a Gilera multi.

Keller set to work building an original chassis. Details of the design are non-existent although a couple of contemporary photographs reveal its eccentricity. From the front, the three-wheeler looked like a racing car as it had two front wheels and the driver obscured the passenger, who sat behind him wedged in a cockpit over the rear wheel. An all-embracing red and white fairing enshrouded the engine. Keller was able to use the power of the Gilera to win a national event at Regensdorf in June and eagerly took the car to the Italian GP at Monza. The off-beat device capsized in a corner at the end of the back straight in practice. The passenger stalked off, having had enough, and no more was seen of Keller's unusual creation.

Fortunately for the faithful in the Monza parkland circuit, Ferruccio had not committed the firm's reputation exclusively to Keller's safe-keeping. He had set Passoni to design an integral chassis, which in truth emerged as a not particularly original concept. The frame and forks were virtually identical to those of the solo, but were shortened. The front wheel measured 3.25 × 18 in., the rear 3.50 × 18 in. and the sidecar 4.00 × 12 in. The chair was a simple platform. The most notable feature was a massive fairing which boxed in the sides and extended around and over the rear wheel, so that the driver literally sat in the bike. Luigi Gilera entrusted the machine to the care of the veteran Albino Milani, with his brother Rossano in the chair.

Despite being last but one away, the Gilera scythed through into an ever-extending lead, setting a record lap around the Monza circuit at 96.78 mph. Capable of 118 mph, the Gilera was about 10 bhp and 10 mph up on the BMW outfits campaigned by Noll and Schneider, who registered a fortunate one–two when the Italian combination suffered a flat tyre when in sight of the flag.

After a lengthy hibernation, the racer re-emerged for the Monza GP in 1956. Passoni

Merlo and Magri on course for the laurels at the Italian GP in 1952. Note the massive brace for the front forks

135

dispensed with the full fairing, as Milani had complained that it caused the engine's heat to roast his legs; a more conventional dustbin was employed. The saddle was extended so that the passenger could put his full weight over the rear wheel. In the race, the Milani brothers outpaced the Munich twins and won by nearly a minute, notching another record lap at 99.63 mph.

Albino Milani admitted that the race was a tedious affair for him, such was the superiority of his engine.

The solitary appearance in 1957 resulted in an even more comprehensive victory. BMW's newly-crowned world champion, Fritz Hillebrand, had been killed in a crash at Bilbao a week before the Italian GP, and stablemate Schneider withdrew from the Monza round in sympathy. This left the Milani brothers completely unchallenged and they rode home over a minute ahead of Cyril Smith, collecting yet another

Albino and Rossano Milani at Monza in 1955, with the fully-faired, redesigned outfit with which they led, only to retire

The Milani brothers, and Luigi Gilera, on the grid at Monza in 1957

record lap with a tour at 100.56 mph.

Official factory participation in the category was not quite over. At the Monza record-breaking sessions in November, 350 cc and 500 cc solo machines were provided with a third wheel, supported by a couple of struts, and thereby transformed into sidecars for record purposes. Initially, Alfredo Milani rode them to standing-start records, but when he departed for South America, brother Albino was asked to establish the long-distance marks. On the 350 cc

Albino Milani on the notional 'outfit', ready for record breaking at Monza in 1957

version, Albino Milani covered over 116 miles in an hour, which was sufficient to take 500 cc, 750 cc and 1200 cc class records into the bargain.

The Gilera sidecar story appeared to be over, and so it might have been but for the persistence of the small bespectacled engineer from Montreux, Florian Camathias. The tiny Swiss, perennial championship runner-up, sought a Deubel-beater in the Italian factories. Rebuffed by MV and Bianchi, he sent his Italian-speaking wife to Arcore to extract a multi for the 1963 season. Alfredo Milani, hearing of this endeavour, also contacted his old master, hoping to install a four in a sidecar outfit. Both attempts were thwarted when Gilera decided to support

Duke's venture. However, when Scuderia Duke folded at season's end, Camathias seized his opportunity, visiting Commendatore Gilera and cajoling an engine for the forthcoming campaign. Similar attempts by Seeley and Vincent to extract a coveted multi met with no response.

Camathias revealed his Gilera-engined outfit at the international Hutchinson 100 meeting in

April. Having cast regular crewman Alfred Herzig from the chair in a wet race, Camathias commandeered Roland Foll as deputy passenger for a subsequent event in which they finished second to Chris Vincent's BMW.

A sleek fairing in traditional Gilera red and white exuded elegance, and a light-alloy dark red panelling shrouding the rear of the machine lent an air of purpose. The heart of the machine was the celebrated four-cylinder engine; although dated, it developed at least ten per cent more power than the works short-stroke Munich

The sleek Gilera-powered sidecar built by Camathias, pictured in 1964 at the top of Church Road, Douglas

twins, which were also beginning to age. The home-made tubular chassis, with an integral sidecar, was an ungainly complex construction, resembling miniature scaffolding.

Similarly home-built, both front and rear forks were pivoted. Front and rear wheels were standard, 16 in. and spoked, and as was customary a smaller 14 in. racing car-type wheel was fitted to the sidecar. All three wheels were hydraulically braked, the front being a disc with twin calipers. Mounted on the sidecar floor was a long, narrow tank from which petrol was lifted to the header tank by a battery-operated electric pump.

An inveterate record breaker, having established world's best times on BMW-, NSU- and Honda-powered sidecars, Camathias took his new outfit to Monza to establish standing-start kilometre records for the 500 cc, 750 cc and 1200 cc classes. Thereafter, he participated in the Austrian GP held on an autobahn circuit near Salzburg, but gearbox gremlins prompted an early retirement. Two days later, although beset with brake problems, he managed second place behind Max Deubel in the Saar GP over the St Wendel street circuit.

On the following weekend, Camathias monopolized the first of the season's classic rounds at the Montjuich Park track. With Foll still in the chair, he won much as he pleased, over 20 seconds clear of Otto Kolle's BMW, to record the last classic victory by the once all-conquering marque.

As so often before, impetuosity was his undoing at the tortuous Clermont-Ferrand circuit. Within sight of victory of the French GP, Camathias over-revved his engine, so that it was all he could do to limp home seventh. The saga of woe was not quite ended—returning from Clermont, he crashed his transporter, bashing his racer and sustaining four cracked ribs.

The three-lap sidecar race opened the 1964 TT programme. Despite the loss of fourth gear, Camathias maintained a lead of five seconds, on corrected time, over Deubel until he overshot Signpost Corner on the first lap. The German stretched his advantage as fuel starvation began to afflict the Gilera. By Ramsey on the final tour the champion had obliterated the starting deficit of 40 seconds and he swept past when the Gilera died at Kate's Cottage. Camathias, having stopped to inspect the engine, restarted only to run into a bank, smashing the screen and further injuring the long-suffering Herzig, newly restored to the chair. The intrepid pair set off once more, coasting and pushing into 15th place, to earn stupendous applause and the final bronze.

Three weeks later at Assen for the Dutch round—a meeting marred by the death of Foll on his 125 cc Honda in practice—Camathias was powerless as Seeley, on the FCS, tore away. The Swiss disputed second place with Vincent for several laps, but his efforts came to a fiery conclusion when petrol was sprayed on to the engine.

At Spa the following weekend, fuel starvation beset the effort on the second lap of the Belgian GP, although after a pit stop he recorded the fastest lap. This was to be the outfit's swan-song; it was never to fire in anger again.

Such was the Camathias rate of attrition that there were no raceworthy Gilera engines available for the remainder of the season, which the Swiss spent on his 1963 FCS. The year ended prematurely and tragically in an accident in August at the Avus international in West Berlin, which knocked Camathias unconscious and resulted in Herzig losing a leg.

Camathias thereafter attempted to borrow, and even to purchase, one of the jealously-preserved multis for a fresh onslaught, but the harassed Gilera staff resented the succession of blown engines, so his pestering was to no avail. The ever-popular Swiss, who was runner-up in the title stakes on no fewer than four occasions, reverted to a BMW-engined outfit on which he crashed fatally at an end-of-season event at Brands Hatch in 1965.

Alfredo Milani was another who attempted to prise an engine out of Arcore for the 1965 season, envisaging a belated return to his early career as a charioteer. He too was eventually rebuffed and with his forlorn attempt Gilera's association with sidecar racing finally petered out.

Florian Camathias and Alfred Herzig round Quarter Bridge in practice for the 1964 Sidecar TT

11 | Scuderia Duke

The prestigious blue-riband championship events were virtually monopolized in 1958, 1959 and 1960 by John Surtees on the metronomic MV, while his erstwhile Gilera adversaries campaigned such second-rate steeds as were available. Duke, after a demoralizing spell on BMW twins, retired from the sport which he had graced for a decade, McIntyre reverted to Joe Potts-prepared singles and Liberati opted for a trusty Saturno.

At the close of the 1960 season, Gilera's general manager, Michele Bianchi, revealed that the parsimonious company had postponed its much-awaited return to the tracks. The announcement prompted Stan Hailwood into immediate action. He flew to Milan in November and turned up at Arcore brandishing an open cheque, offering to buy the entire race shop. When this extravagant offer was rejected, he attempted to procure the use of two of the priceless multis for Mike and Bob McIntyre for the 1961 season. This effort was also doomed to, and duly met with, failure.

By 1962, Commendatore Gilera's long-suppressed enthusiasm had been rekindled, as he was constantly pestered by the likes of Liberati and Milani. Works participation seemed imminent when, in March 1962, fate dealt a harsh blow. Libero Liberati habitually practised over local roads around Terni on his private road-going Saturno. On one such outing, he skidded on the exposed rails of a level crossing that had been made slippery by a shower of rain. He hit a

Far right **The Gilera race shop in 1962—untouched since 1957**

142

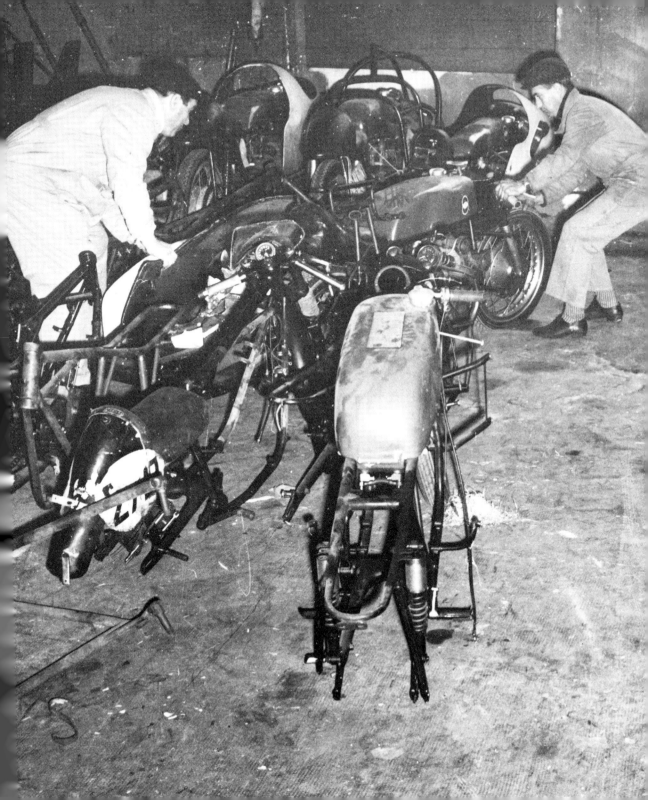

wall and died shortly afterwards. Gilera's hopes now rested with McIntyre but, despairing of extracting a decision from the dithering potentates in Arcore, he had signed for the burgeoning Honda empire.

Above **Patrignani and Giuseppe Gilera, together with a multi, in 1962**

Left **Passoni shows off a dust-laden multi awaiting rebirth**

Tragically, the universally admired Scot sustained fatal injuries in an Oulton Park crash in August. The Remembrance meeting at the same circuit some weeks later featured demonstration laps by a cluster of celebrities, including Duke aboard a dustbin-faired Gilera. Ironically, this was to be the prelude to the marque's competitive renaissance.

John Hartle rode the multi at Oulton prior to the meeting and it was entrusted to Derek Minter for a tyre-testing session at Mallory Park, where

The Gilera reawakens in the hands of John Hartle at Brands Hatch in 1963. Note the makeshift fairing

he came within a second of the lap record. This was the opening Duke had been impatiently waiting for; he now obtained machines for a romp at Monza early in 1963 to assess prospects.

Minter was the obvious choice to put the dust-laden bike through its paces. He had been at the peak of his form in 1962 when he had pointedly ignored Honda team orders to ride to a splendid 250 cc TT victory on a tired Hondis Ltd-entered 1961 model. The second string was Hartle, who boasted experience of a fearsome multi from his days as an Agusta runner.

Enzo Ferrari had masterminded a motorcycle racing team in pre-war days. He formed a friendship with Giuseppe Gilera that was strengthened in later years when they shared the grief of losing an only son. Gilera had helped out the Maranello factory when the controversial 1½-litre limit was introduced for Formula 1 in 1961. The Prancing Horse équipe now reciprocated by assisting with the preparation of 500 cc and 350 cc engines for the Monza tests.

Scuderia Duke's number one, Derek Minter, riding to an early-season success at Brands Hatch

The new dolphin fairings were fibreglass Bill Jakeman jobs. As riding techniques had changed over the last five years, wads of foam were taped to the backrests of the seats so that the two riders could sit further forward and lean more when cornering. Severe fog and ice delayed and ultimately hampered the tests.

Although the 350 cc bike was way off the Monza pace, the senior model appeared to be competitive and Commendatore Gilera willingly gave the go-ahead for a comeback, despite some misgivings in the boardroom. The effort was essentially private. Duke's reputation was sufficient to obtain finance from Castrol and Avon and he negotiated starting money for his riders. The factory's contribution was restricted to the bikes and the provision of mechanics, primarily the faithful Giovanni Fumagalli and Luigi Colombo; Giuseppe Gilera was not about to unveil the engine's secrets to prying outsiders.

Ominously, some needless friction arose at this early stage in the proceedings when the factory, unbeknown to Duke, approached Hailwood for his signature, which was, however, to be appended to an Agusta contract.

The Scuderia Duke enterprise materialized in April, when Minter rode to a handsome victory at Silverstone, although Hartle struggled to fend off the eager young Phil Read. Minter immediately sensed a problem with the front suspension, which had been strengthened years earlier to cope with the pressure created by, and indeed the weight of, the now discarded dustbin fairing. Minter suggested experimenting with the swinging-arm in order to transfer weight and was more than a little irritated when Duke chose to ignore him and test a range of shock-absorber fluids in search of an answer. Fortunately, internal dissensions were assuaged by Minter's victories at Brands Hatch and Oulton Park before enthusiastic crowds of 60,000, anxious to savour the sight and sound of the legendary Arcore multis.

Confrontation with the Gallarate squad, now restored to full-blooded works status after two seasons of notionally 'Privat' participation, was eagerly anticipated. The big showdown came at the Imola Gold Cup, when Minter and Hartle humbled the peerless Hailwood and his back-up rider, new recruit Silvio Grassetti.

Although suffering from a troublesome wrist injury, Hailwood made no excuses, admitting that Minter's riding had been unmatchable. The Oxford Flyer estimated that top speed and braking of the Gilera and the MV were on a par, but he thought that the former had a noticeable edge in acceleration, especially Hartle's bike. Minter was another to observe, with some disgust, that Hartle was favoured with the faster engine. Remonstrating with Luigi Colombo was to no avail and so in the race Minter had to outbrake his team-mate consistently in order to make his point. Erroneously or otherwise, the King of Brands, who was not given to toeing a works line, now formed the fixed opinion that Duke and Hartle, as northerners of long-standing acquaintance, were deliberately isolating him, the presumptuous southerner.

Minter's grievances were not confined to personal matters; he resented the fact that Duke paid no heed to his recommendations. After riding the 350 cc model in practice at Imola, he requested that the footrests be lifted. Both Colombo and Duke insisted that there had been no grounding in 1957 and were not over-impressed by his suggestion that, with a dolphin fairing and improved tyres, cornering speeds had doubtless increased over the years. Once racing, he had to ride to the limit to overtake Remo Venturi on the bulky Bianchi and, having done so, he duly fell off when a footrest grounded! Minter was understandably aggrieved, while Hartle finished well down on the veteran Italian.

Hartle splashes through Parliament Square, Ramsey, during the wet Junior TT

At Imola, the machines appeared in ultra-light thin magnesium-alloy fairings with sponge-padded knee rests. There were also new carburettor connections, but otherwise the bikes remained essentially in 1957 guise.

Disaster befell Minter in May when he suffered broken vertebrae in the infamous crash at Brands Hatch that killed Dave Downer. With the championship series beckoning, Duke hastily sought a suitable replacement and found him in Phil Read, Senior Manx GP winner in 1960 and Junior TT victor a year later.

The reconstituted team's title challenge commenced with the 350 cc race at Hocken-heim. Hartle soon retired with vibration problems, leaving Read trailing in the wake of Redman's Honda and Venturi. Technically, the 350 cc class had moved on of late, particularly with the entry of the four-valve Hondas, and the Gilera was rendered practically obsolete. Read recalls the bike with a combination of pity and horror: 'It was irritating enough being left behind by the leaders, but eventually Tommy Robb on his 305 cc Honda twin steamed by on the straight; the bikes should have been pensioned off immediately.' Read's third place ahead of Havel's Jawa was indicative of the machine's limited capabilities.

Three 350 cc bikes were taken across the Irish Sea for the Junior TT. One engine blew up in practice and Read's gave up the ghost on the second lap of the race. Hartle soldiered on gamely and inherited a remote second place behind the Rhodesian champion when Hailwood's MV expired. Despite losing a cylinder when the incessant rain took its toll on the last lap, he clung on to the six championship points.

Hailwood mounted a formidable challenge for the Senior TT, pointedly completing every practice lap at over the magic 100 mph. Hartle's

Phil Read negotiates Governor's Bridge on his way to third place in the Senior TT

impressive opening tour at 105.5 mph was of no avail, for he was caught on the roads by his rival, who turned in a blistering record-breaking 106.3 mph circuit. Mike the Bike eventually won the Trophy, a minute ahead of the Gilera team leader.

Hartle's first lap had been considerably faster than McIntyre's best speed in 1957, but it should

Hartle aboard the 500 cc machine on which he was runner-up to the maestro Hailwood in the Island

be remembered that Hartle had been scratching, riding into the gutters and banks on a couple of occasions as he struggled to fend off the rampant Hailwood. The relatively inexperienced Read

The still-mighty four-cylinder engine pictured in the Isle of Man in 1963

admitted to being plain scared by the novelty of riding an unmanageable bike over the unforgiving Mountain course, yet despite suffering a malfunctioning cylinder, he averaged over 100 mph to collect a fine third place.

Scuderia Duke's fortunes revived at the Dutch TT, where, having ditched the 350 cc project, five 500 cc bikes were available. Hailwood's MV spluttered on to two cylinders shortly after the start, enabling Hartle and Read to register an unchallenged one–two.

By the time of the Belgian GP at Spa, Read was questioning the wisdom of his elevation to much-vaunted works status. He was undoubtedly impressed with the potent engine and explains: 'There was no sudden rush as I had expected but instead there was usable power, and lots of it, from 8000 rpm. The problem, of course, was with the handling, which was too light at the front end. Not much pressure could be applied to the handlebars, which meant that

Minter, Hailwood and Hartle after the Ulster GP, won by the MV rider

the Gilera had to be banked over far earlier than my Norton. Also, the frames were very variable and certainly needed their steering dampers.'

Read also found that Duke was prone to criticizing his riding ability: 'He was watching me in practice at Stavelot and tore me off afterwards for my cornering and gearchanging. Doing this in public in the pits was not particularly confidence-boosting.' All in all, the ambitious Read was increasingly frustrated, believing that Gilera's effort was hopelessly underfinanced and lacked a presiding mechanical genius such as MV enjoyed in Arturo Magni. Nevertheless, he came home second at Spa, behind Hailwood, with whom he now shared the championship lead.

At this stage, Minter returned to the fold, testing the bike at Monza. He broke the lap record unofficially, but then lost the front forks when braking from 100 mph; a bolt had not been tightened properly and had worked loose. Uninjured, he was able to win his comeback race at Oulton Park, turning in a record lap.

Hailwood emphasized his and the MV's all too evident superiority at the Ulster GP, recording the first series of 100 mph laps of the Dundrod course to beat Hartle. Minter, upset by a further difference of opinion with Duke regarding faulty boat bookings, trailed home a distant third, dispirited as the bumpy circuit aggravated his already painful back. Before the race, Duke announced to the assembled press that he expected Hartle and Minter to challenge for the lead and that he hoped Read would perform respectably. This honest if unwisely expressed appraisal of his riders' prospects stung Read into riding beyond the limit. He dug a footrest in at Leathemstown on the second lap and duly stepped off, hurting his back in the process.

One telling statistic emerged from the flying kilometre trap at Dundrod; the MV clocked 143.5 mph, whereas the best Gilera, Minter's, could summon no more than 138 mph.

Hailwood was simply unbeatable at Sachsen-ring, home of the East German GP, with victories in the 250 cc, 350 cc and 500 cc classes. Although Hartle came to grief, Minter salvaged second place in the Senior event. A solitary Gilera remained unscathed after the recent prangs; it was accorded to Hartle for the Finnish GP at Tampere, but gearbox problems jinxed his effort. Hailwood, needless to say, dominated the race.

The revised cylinder head which Passoni had designed in anticipation of the 1958 season was now pressed into service on Minter's bike for the crucial Italian GP. It sported deeper finning to assist cooling and was slab-sided to reduce width. Unfortunately, its adoption necessitated time-consuming modifications to the carburet-tors, frame and tank, diverting attention from the other machines.

Hartle's competitive Gilera career came to an unscheduled conclusion when he hit the Monza tarmac at 130 mph during practice; he incurred only superficial injuries, but the bike was wrecked. In the race, the Gilera riders were humiliated by Hailwood and Venturi. Read pulled out when huge uncontrollable slides materia-lized; the nut attaching the gearchange linkage to the gearbox shaft was too tight to allow for expansion of the crankcase when the engine was warm, causing the pedal to stick in fourth gear. Minter realized he was on a loser when Venturi motored past him; badly-machined internals in the new gearbox and an oil leakage brought his challenge to an untimely end. It was this unmitigated fiasco, on home territory, rather than the string of disappointments throughout the season, which incurred the intense dis-pleasure of the Gilera factory management and sounded the death knell to Duke's project.

The squad did not travel for the Argentinian GP, which fell, inevitably, to Hailwood ahead of a host of local riders including, in third place, one Benedicto Caldarella. At season's end, Hartle and Read were third and fourth in the title standings, ousted from runner-up spot by privateer Alan Shepherd on his Matchless.

Derek Minter drops his multi at Scarborough in 1963

The team did, however, compete in the remaining home internationals. At Scarborough, Minter unceremoniously dropped his mount on loose gravel at Mere Hairpin and Read notched his solitary race victory on a Gilera. Having recorded a couple of successes at Brands, Minter was roundly beaten by Hailwood in the money-spinning Race of the Year at Mallory.

In October, Duke arranged for Hartle to test the bike with a leading-link front fork, designed by Ken Sprayson, at Monza. The disillusioned factory staff were not convinced that Duke should run next year's show and independently invited Hailwood, Venturi and new-sensation Giacomo Agostini to test the machine. Understandably, MV, Bianchi and Morini respectively would not release their stars and so a handful of promising riders were given a run-out, including Renzo Rossi of Bianchi, and Alberto Pagani and Gilberto Milani of Aermacchi, without justifying a contract.

Duke was hoping to arrange an Australasian tour over the winter for either Hartle or Alan Shepherd, but he notified Minter that his services would no longer be required. Duke's grandiose plans were brought to nought for, at the end of the year, Gilera's grandson Massimo Lucchini, who had attempted to liaise between the English squad and the factory personnel, informed Duke that the machines would not be made available to him for 1964.

12 | The twilight years

By 1964 motorcycle production at the Arcore plant, ravaged by persistent industrial disputes, was down to a pathetic trickle. As the once-proud Gilera company lingered on without conviction, nourished only by fading memories of past glories, so too did the outdated 500 cc racer. Nevertheless, such was the charisma of the machine that a host of star riders clamoured for the opportunity to race it. Of these, only the tiny Argentinian Benedicto Caldarella was to enhance his reputation by mounting a serious if truncated challenge to the MV stranglehold.

Caldarella's brief but impressive career began in 1959 aboard his father's Saturno, which carried him to a national title. He repeated this success in 1963, by which time he was working in Gilera's factory in Buenos Aires. As a publicity stunt, one of the ex-Scuderia Duke machines was sent over for his use in November 1963. His victories in four notionally international races against modest opposition were doubtless virtually inevitable, but less predictable was that, in winning the prestigious Ferruccio Gilera event in Buenos Aires, he broke the lap record established by none other than Hailwood with his mighty MV.

Thus encouraged, Caldarella and mechanic Fumagalli decided to try their luck at the early-season GP at Daytona. Hailwood prefaced the race by riding his spare MV to the classic hour record over the banked track, marginally upping McIntyre's 1957 speed. In the afternoon he had a stiffer task, discovering that the Gilera's acceleration left the MV in its wake on the fast banked

Far right **Benedicto Caldarella and Giovanni Fumagalli at Daytona in 1964**

Caldarella aboard the ex-Scuderia Duke multi in the 500 cc GP at Daytona

Back in Italy, the veteran Alfredo Milani eventually cajoled a multi out of Commendatore Gilera, but in the first race of the national season at Modena he lagged well behind Venturi on Lino Tonti's revised Bianchi and MV's reserve pilot Mendogni.

sections of the course. Only by outriding the Argentinian in the swervery could the world champion stay with him. Regrettably, Caldarella's effort was foiled by the onset of gearbox troubles at half-distance.

Caldarella with a short-lived lead over Mike Hailwood (MV) in the 1964 American classic

Caldarella arrived in Italy in April. Sadly, he was not to receive anything like a full-scale back-up. His crew generally consisted of no more than his father and a solitary factory mechanic, trundling around Europe in a rickety van. Indeed, his arrival coincided with a series of debilitating strikes at the Arcore base which necessitated Caldarella and his mechanic clambering over walls and gates in the dead of night to snatch much-needed spare parts from the race shop.

Against this calamitous background, his performance in winning the Imola Gold Cup with lap and race records was little short of phenomenal, despite Hailwood's absence. Milani's ride was also encouraging, for he had shadowed Caldarella and Venturi until the now-familiar gearbox malaise set in. However, the 40-year-old realized that the years had taken their toll, not only on him but on the machines: 'I had talked Gilera, against his better judgement, into giving me a bike, but I was looking after it without factory assistance and it was simply an impossible task. The bikes were still fast but the engines were very tired. Two engines blew up on me in practice at Imola and then mechanical problems ruined my race.' The machine's once-fabled reliability had deserted.

Caldarella, aged 24, called 'Chi che', was now hailed by the press, a shade prematurely, as both a natural and a pretender to Hailwood's throne. He had available the bike produced for Minter at the previous year's Italian GP, with the revised cylinder head, but new parts were not to be forthcoming. Indeed, the factory's slender resources were to be stretched beyond the limit as the season progressed, for the effervescent Camathias abused engines with alarming and unendearing frequency.

The tiny Argentinian sensation seemed to have received his come-uppance at Cesenatico, where he trailed home a distant third behind Hailwood and Venturi. Milani was a disgruntled fourth, with which he concluded his distinguished career. Proposals to enter the TT with Caldarella and Hartle, the latter on a bike to be loaned to Duke, were thwarted by continuing labour problems in Arcore, so it was not until Assen that Caldarella was able to re-enter the title lists. He clung pluckily to Hailwood for a couple of laps by dint of overimpetuous riding. Unscheduled excursions on to the grass and a violent tank-slapper convinced the challenger that he was overdoing it and the MV gradually pulled away. After eight laps, the temperamental Gilera engine expired. The sorry tale was repeated at the Belgian round; Caldarella was losing two seconds a lap to Hailwood when the rigours of the punishing Masta straight proved too much for the frail motor.

A brace of successes at Vallelunga and San Remo resuscitated the half-baked enterprise, but a foot injury, sustained in practice at San Remo, ruled Caldarella out of both the German rounds of the championship and then the Ulster.

The Italian GP prompted a renewed, if unspectacular, effort from the factory. Silvio Grassetti was recruited on a one-off basis and new fairings, with cooling vents, were conjured up. Alas, Hailwood's meteoric getaway from the Monza grid foiled Caldarella's proposed stream-lining tactics, but the Gilera lasted the full distance for once and finished a mere ten seconds down on the MV. The Argentinian was also credited, possibly erroneously, with the fastest lap, but Grassetti's model failed him early on.

At the end of the season, Massimo Lucchini, who had been running the show, resumed his studies, leaving the factory's racing effort without any guiding hand. In a forlorn attempt to revive the company's jaded fortunes, Lino Tonti was signed up to develop production machines. Unfortunately, Caldarella and Luigi Colombo returned to South America for a winter tour and

Minter and Colombo with two of the latest seven-speed models at the Isle of Man in 1966

were thereby denied the opportunity to liaise with Tonti, whose involvement with the racing world embraced not only his spell at Bianchi but also a partnership with Giuseppe Pattoni of Paton fame. In any event, Tonti's engagement with Gilera appears not to have been an unqualified success and he was soon to depart for Mandello, where he was responsible for the development of Guzzi's successful V-twin range.

The dire financial situation precluded a racing programme in 1965, but in 1966 the organizers of the Italian championship meetings made extravagant offers to Gilera, and indeed to Guzzi, to wheel out their celebrated machinery. So it was that Remo Venturi—now 40 years old—joined the Arcore ranks to compete in domestic events, with Luigi Colombo, Giovanni Fumagalli and his nephew Mario constituting the team of mechanics. Tonti proposed a slimmer fairing and a new gearbox, which was to have six and finally seven speeds. Disc brakes were also mooted, but they never materialized; however, the duplex front brakes, first tested in 1957, were re-introduced.

Venturi rendered yeoman if modest service, making the best of what was by now a distinctly bad job—second at Modena to Agostini's 350 cc MV, first at Riccione after Ago crashed and a faller in torrential rain at Milano Marittima.

The Imola Gold Cup witnessed the return to the Gilera saga of Derek Minter, who was invited to try his hand after he outsped Venturi in practice on his Norton single. He found that the bike had taken a couple of backward steps over the previous three years; the gears kept jumping and the suspension was rock hard. Nevertheless, he managed to keep Agostini in sight in the race until clutch slip set in. Venturi, meanwhile, succumbed to plug trouble.

At Cesenatico, Minter rode the new seven-speeder, which sported a wasp-waisted fairing, but his race was curtailed by front fork problems while Venturi's effort was foiled by gearbox troubles. The next round of the Italian title was held at San Remo and heralded the return to European competition of Benedicto Caldarella. Unfortunately, he was scooped by a gust of high wind along the sea-front during practice; he fell, suffering a broken collarbone, and his challenge was over before it had started. Venturi salvaged another second place behind Agostini.

Minter's worldly-wise suspicion was that the bureaucrats within the organization were not genuinely interested in racing but were simply sending the bikes along to pocket the proffered generous appearance money. On one occasion, he tested the seven-speed machine over a short circuit at Modena that he had never ridden before and which was covered in loose gravel. First time out he rode to within one second of Agostini's record; he argued that with further practice this time could be whittled down, but the Gilera personnel, dispirited by the failure to match the MV's speed immediately, packed up for home, much to his evident disgust.

Convinced that, with perseverance, the Gilera was a potential winner, Minter took two racers, both seven-speed models, to the Island for the TT, delayed that year by the seamen's strike. This was a private venture, paid for by the King of Brands, organized with the aid of journalist and Gilera enthusiast Charlie Rous. Gilera's contribution comprised Luigi Colombo to fettle the engines.

After a week of undistinguished practice times, the bike was written off by the pontificating scribes; Minter, however, remained confident. In fact, the machines were afflicted with faulty suspension as the Girling units had no rebound damping. It was not until the final practice session on Saturday morning that replacements arrived. Minter recalls the one lap he enjoyed that morning: 'I took it easy for the first few miles and then poured it on. The bicycle had higher gearing than Hartle's in 1963 and it was moving as fast as anything ever had over the course. On the drop from the Creg to Brandish I reckon I must have been approaching 160 mph.'

Unfortunately, there had been a brief shower at Brandish and Minter was the first to arrive on the scene. Down he went, fracturing a wrist and concluding, ignominiously, Gilera's glorious association with the TT.

Similarly unsatisfactory was Venturi's foray at the Italian GP. Of the two machines available, one had a restyled petrol tank in a dark metallic maroon. A crestfallen Venturi wound up third after practice, well off the pace set by Agostini and Hailwood, and after some harsh and doubtless noisy words his entry was withdrawn.

The two bikes, by now sporting grey and black fairings and duplex front brakes, were then packed off for the end-of-season international at Brands Hatch. Venturi appropriated the faster

Charlie Rous, Luigi Colombo and Frank Perris pictured at the Race of the South meeting in 1966, the Gilera team's final competitive outing in Britain

Left **Perris and Venturi with the restyled multi, now boasting a maroon tank and a grey and black fairing, but doomed to mid-table oblivion**

Above **Ex-Suzuki teamster Perris acquaints himself with the four-stroke multi**

Perris, in an undistinguished midfield position, fends off Griff Jenkins during the 1966 Race of the South

model while, in Minter's enforced absence, the other was offered to the promising Peter Williams. Pertinently, he declined the double-edged opportunity on the grounds that his Arter

Matchless was as rapid. Thus, the former Suzuki star Frank Perris was allocated a weekend on the antique multi. In both the 500 cc Redex Trophy and the 1000 cc Race of the South, Venturi and Perris mixed it with the privateers, finishing in undignified midfield positions. Perris concluded that the Gilera was as fast, but not as

manageable, as the 350 cc Benelli that he had tested recently.

This harsh opinion was borne out at Vallelunga, scene of the final round of the Italian

The 40-year-old Venturi, formerly of MV and Bianchi, made the best of a bad job, but he too languished into mediocrity at Brands Hatch. Note the new front brake

championship. Venturi opted to ride the older five-speed model in what was to be the four-cylinder machine's final competitive sortie. Despite Agostini falling off, a victim of the inclement weather, Venturi had to be content with his habitual runner-up spot, behind Renzo Pasolini aboard the Benelli multi. With this unmemorable episode, Gilera's official participation in the sport limped to a belated conclusion.

Both Minter and Perris were angling for a Gilera ride in 1967. Unable to prise information out of Arcore, Minter visited Commendatore Gilera. The venerable old man, conscious as ever of rider safety, had been upset by Minter's TT injury, not to mention mortified by the équipe's miserable showing against the new generation of Italian multis and Japanese exotica. He finally cried enough and told Minter that the machines would return in perpetuity to the grubby cellar from which they had emerged, with such disappointing results, in 1963. Thus, the 500 cc four-cylinder Gilera, arguably the most glamorous and successful of all racing motorcycles, came to the end of the distinguished line.

13 | Epilogue

Twenty years have now passed since Gilera Grand Prix racers roamed the world's racetracks. The two decades have witnessed the onslaught of Oriental two-stroke technology, the decline and ultimate capitulation of the four-stroke engine, the integration and dominance of a breed of poker-faced racers from the New World, the demise of genuine road circuits and the onset of tobacco mega-sponsorship. However, such is the enduring appeal of the Gilera name that unsubstantiated reports of the marque's imminent return to the tracks have cropped up over these turbulent years with unrelieved monotony.

Throughout the late 1960s a myth persisted that a brand-new 250 cc machine was on the stocks, to be ridden by Agostini, Pasolini or Carruthers, depending on which rumour-mongering journal was peddling the story. That the proposed comeback, if such there was, did not materialize was hardly surprising when viewed against the backcloth of the company's desperate financial plight. Production at the strife-torn Arcore plant was down to a meagre 350 motorcycles per month. Of the workforce of 550, over half were on short time and permanent closure must have seemed imminent when a receiver was appointed in 1968.

A saviour emerged in the shape of the mammoth Piaggio organization, producer of the ubiquitous Vespa. Concerned by dwindling scooter sales, Piaggio decided to diversify by taking a stall in the motorcycle market-place. In purchasing Gilera, lock, stock and barrel, in late 1969, Piaggio acquired not only the Arcore factory, which may have been of dubious worth, but, more importantly, a renowned name of international repute.

With the proceeds of the sale, a rumoured £2 million, to his credit, Commendatore Gilera finally retired. A truly civilized, almost Renaissance, man of many parts, musician, sailor, huntsman, Giuseppe Gilera died on 21 November 1971, a few months after another colossus of his era, Count Domenico Agusta.

One last bid to winkle a 500 cc multi out of the Arcore mausoleum was proffered by John Blanchard, who proposed to act as team manager with Ray Pickrell as rider. After the obligatory spell of customary Italianate ambivalence, Piaggio ultimately shut the door on his project.

When the company had been firmly re-established on a viable commercial basis, its competition department was revived and a successful motocross squad engendered. As the wish fathers the thought, so this led to speculation that a Grand Prix rebirth was on the cards.

The incessant fictions of Gilera's impending return to the 500 cc category have sufficed to fill numerous columns in the gossip pages of the motorcycle journals. The contribution in 1979 was that Minarelli's two-stroke wizard Jorg Muller was to be engaged. Three years later, a similarly baseless fable surfaced that Suzuki Italia's mastermind Roberto Gallina was to be recruited to organize a squad, which was to be based on the ailing Sanvenero enterprise. Another yarn of the early 1980s was that a disc-valved square

four had been designed by the motocross team's engineer, Jan Witteveen, but he sloped off to the shores of Lake Varese to work for the go-ahead Cagiva concern. To add a touch of the exotic, a four-cylinder turbocharged 250 cc engine formed the centrepiece of 1984's tales.

In fact, the competition department at Arcore operates under conditions of the strictest secrecy. Even the public relations staff at the factory are not privy to its projects, which are certainly not for retail to the press, who are left to wallow in their imaginative offerings.

For the sake of completeness it should, however, be recorded that the hallowed name Gilera was once again seen on the racetracks in 1984. Piaggio, substantial importers into Spain, negotiated a deal to sponsor up-and-coming Sito Pons in his Grand Prix campaign, and so it was that a Gilera decal was affixed to the petrol tank of his Rotax-engined 250 cc Kobas.

That unspectacular sortie apart, Piaggio, on behalf of its better-known subsidiary, has consistently eschewed Grand Prix competition. Instead, enthusiasts' have to be satisfied with an occasional glimpse of the ageing Gilera racers, which are wheeled out of the factory's private museum from time to time. The illustrious multis are unveiled for publicity runs at Monza to coincide with the launch of new models and displayed at Misano's annual Historic GP. But perhaps most memory-jerking have been Duke's demonstration outings aboard a dolphin-faired model over the Mountain course. His nostalgia-provoking rides in the TT Classic laps in 1979 and 1981 have offered, for however short a time, a sight and sound of arguably the most charismatic machine of road racing's Golden Age.

Appendix One
Classic victories

(1) 1937–46 500 cc four-cylinder

1937 Italian GP (Monza)—Aldrighetti

1939 Swedish GP (Saxtorp)—Serafini
     German GP (Sachsenring)—Serafini
     Ulster GP (Clady)—Serafini

1946 Swiss GP (Geneva)—Pagani

(2) 1940–57 500 cc Saturno

1947 Italian GP (Milan)—Artesiani

(3) 1948–53 500 cc four-cylinder

1948 Italian GP (Faenza)—Masserini

1949 Dutch TT (Assen)—Pagani
     Italian GP (Monza)—Pagani

1950 Belgian GP (Spa)—Masetti
     Dutch TT (Assen)—Masetti

1951 Spanish GP (Montjuich)—Masetti
     French GP (Albi)—Milani
     Italian GP (Monza)—Milani

1952 Dutch TT (Assen)—Masetti
     Belgian GP (Spa)—Masetti
     Ulster GP (Clady)—McCandless

1953 Dutch TT (Assen)—Duke
     Belgian GP (Spa)—Milani
     French GP (Rouen)—Duke
     Swiss GP (Berne)—Duke
     Italian GP (Monza)—Duke

(4) 1954–66 500 cc four-cylinder

1954 French GP (Reims)—Monneret, P.
     Belgian GP (Spa)—Duke
     Dutch TT (Assen)—Duke
     German GP (Solitude)—Duke
     Swiss GP (Berne)—Duke
     Italian GP (Monza)—Duke

1955 Spanish GP (Montjuich)—Armstrong
     French GP (Reims)—Duke
     TT–Mountain—Duke
     German GP (Nürburgring)—Duke
     Belgian GP (Spa)—Colnago
     Dutch TT (Assen)—Duke

1956 German GP (Solitude)—Armstrong
     Italian GP (Monza)—Duke

1957 German GP (Hockenheim)—Liberati
     TT–Mountain—McIntyre
     Ulster GP (Dundrod)—Liberati
     Italian GP (Monza)—Liberati

1963 Dutch TT (Assen)—Hartle

(5) 1956–57 125 cc two-cylinder

1956 German GP (Solitude)—Ferri

(6) 1956–63 350 cc four-cylinder

1956 Italian GP (Monza)—Liberati

1957 German GP (Hockenheim)—Liberati
     TT–Mountain—McIntyre
     Italian GP (Monza)—McIntyre

(7) Sidecars: four-cylinder

1949 Italian GP (Monza)—Frigerio/Ricotti

1951 Swiss GP (Berne)—Frigerio/Ricotti
     Italian GP (Monza)—Milani/Pizzocri

1952 Swiss GP (Berne)—Milani/Pizzocri
     Italian GP (Monza)—Merlo/Magri

1956 Italian GP (Monza)—Milani/Milani, R.

1957 Italian GP (Monza)—Milani/Milani, R.

1964 Spanish GP (Montjuich)—Camathias/Foll

Note: Of the Milani brothers, Alfredo recorded the solo victories listed above. Albino registered the sidecar successes, passengered in 1956 and 1957 by Rossano.

Appendix Two
Existing works racing motorcycles

Model	Number originally built	Existing model	Present whereabouts
A 1935 CNA	Six complete bikes	None	
B 1937–46 500 cc four	At least three racers, plus the record breaker	(1) 1939 solo	In Gilera Museum
		(2) 1939 record breaker	In Gilera Museum
		(3) Post-war sidecar	Probably stolen from Gilera after 1950
C 1948–53 500 cc four	Probably about a dozen complete machines, but they were modified at the end of every season	None	
D 1954–66 500 cc four	Probably about 11 complete machines, but again they were butchered consistently	(1) Hotchpot of mid-1950s styles	In the automobile museum of Turin—'Carlo Biscaretti di Ruffia'
		(2) 1957 guise with dustbin fairing	In the Milan Science Museum
		(3) 1964 guise	In Buenos Aires: ex-Caldarella, retained by Gilera Argentina in 1964
		(4) 1964 guise	In Gilera Museum
		(5) 1966 guise	In Gilera Museum
		(6) 1966 guise	In Gilera Museum
		(7, 8 and 9)	In private ownership in Italy; at least one having been acquired by dubious means
E 1956–57 125 cc twin	Three frames—four engines	(1) In 1967 guise with dolpin fairing	In Gilera Museum
F 1957 175 cc twin	Ten complete machines	(1) In 1957 guise	In Gilera Museum
		(2) In modified form, with dolphin fairing	With Angelo Molteni of Arcore
		(3)	In private ownership in Italy; again, of dubious legality

Model	Number originally built	Existing model	Present whereabouts
G 1949–57 Sidecars	Four or five special frames	(1) In 1957 guise, without fairing	In Gilera Museum
H 1956–57 350 cc four	Four or five complete machines	None	

Note: Apart from the machines retained in the private factory museum in Arcore, Gilera retain an assortment of frames, engines and fairings. In particular, the shell of one of the two Saturno dohc engines languishes in the factory, and it is believed that the supercharged 250 cc four-cylinder engine of 1940 is also hiding in the depths of a cellar in the factory.

Two 175 cc racers were taken on tour to Argentina in 1963–64 and could well have been retained by Gilera Argentina, which was subsequently nationalized.

Dorino Serafini pictured at the Misano Historic GP in 1984 with the 1939 European championship-winning Gilera

The supercharged engine produced somewhere in the
region of 70 bhp, although Gilera's claims are open to
doubt

A 1957 dustbin-faired 500 cc model languishing in the
Milan Science Museum. It is possible that this was the
model used by McIntyre at the Isle of Man

Above **A recently restored 500 cc multi, which is nearest to those used at the tail-end of 1966**

Right **The remnants of Passoni's dohc Saturno engine**

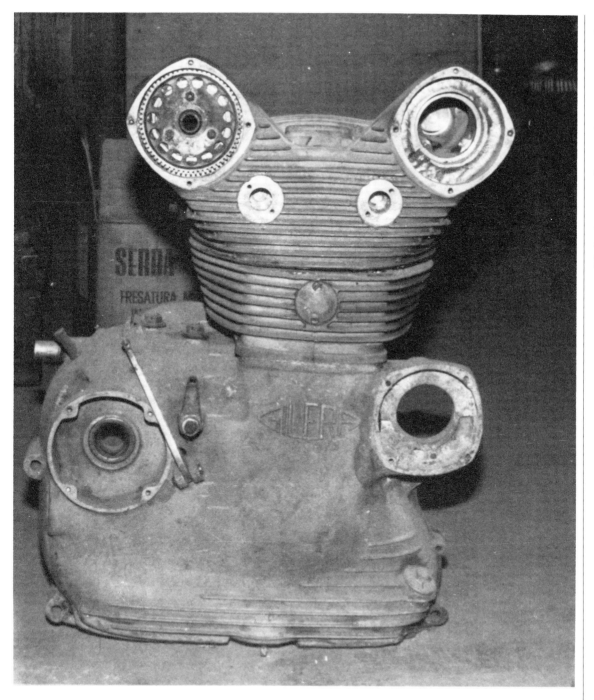

Left The sad remains of one of the 125 cc racers

Above The one remaining working example of the 1957 175 cc twin, although it is not in its original form

The 175 cc engine of the complete model retained by
Gilera in Arcore

The main entrance to the Gilera factory in Arcore

Index

186

The Collector's Library

A complete list of Osprey motorcycle titles is listed overleaf

OSPREY COLLECTOR'S LIBRARY

AJS and Matchless – The Postwar Models
Roy Bacon
0 85045 536 7   **£9.95**

Ariel – The Postwar Models
Roy Bacon
0 85045 537 5   **£9.95**

BMW Twins and Singles
Roy Bacon
0 85045 699 1   **£9.95**

BSA Gold Star and Other Singles
Roy Bacon
0 85045 447 6   **£8.95**

BSA Twins & Triples
Roy Bacon
0 85045 368 2   **£8.95**

Classic British Scramblers
Don Morley
0 85045 649 5   **£9.95**

Classic British Trials Bikes
Don Morley
0 85045 545 6   **£8.95**

Classic Motorcycle Racer Tests
Alan Cathcart
0 85045 589 8   **£8.95**

Ducati Singles
Mick Walker
0 85045 605 3   **£8.95**

Ducati Twins
Mick Walker
0 85045 634 7   **£9.95**

Honda – The Early Classic Motorcycles
Roy Bacon
0 85045 596 0   **£8.95**

Kawasaki – Sunrise to Z1
Roy Bacon
0 85045 544 8   **£8.95**

Military Motorcycles of World War 2
Roy Bacon
0 85045 618 5   **£8.95**

Moto Guzzi Twins
Mick Walker
0 85045 650 9   **£9.95**

MV Agusta
Mick Walker
0 85045 711 4   **£9.95**

Norton Singles
Roy Bacon
0 85045 485 9   **£8.95**

Norton Twins
Roy Bacon
0 85045 423 9   **£8.95**

Royal Enfield – The Postwar Models
Roy Bacon
0 85045 459 X   **£8.95**

Spanish Post-war Road and Racing Motorcycles
Mick Walker
0 85045 705 X   **£9.95**

Suzuki Two-Strokes
Roy Bacon
0 85045 588 X   **£8.95**

Triumph Singles
Roy Bacon
0 85045 566 9   **£6.95**

Triumph Twins & Triples
Roy Bacon
0 85045 700 9   **£9.95**

Velocette Flat Twins
Roy Bacon
0 85045 632 0   **£6.95**

Villiers Singles & Twins
Roy Bacon
0 85045 486 7   **£8.95**

Vincent Vee Twins
Roy Harper
0 85045 435 2   **£8.95**

Yamaha Dirtbikes
Colin MacKellar
0 85045 660 6   **£9.95**

Yamaha Two-Stroke Twins
Colin MacKellar
0 85045 582 0   **£8.95**

OSPREY COLOUR SERIES

Cult of the Harley-Davidson
Gerald Foster
0 85045 463 8   **£6.95**

Harley-Davidson – the cult lives on
Gerald Foster
0 85045 577 4   **£6.95**

Italian Motorcycles
Tim Parker
0 85045 576 6   **£6.95**

Japanese 100hp/11 sec./ 150mph Motorcycles
Tim Parker
0 85045 647 9   **£6.95**

RESTORATION SERIES

BSA Twin Restoration
Roy Bacon
0 85045 699 X   **£12.95**

Norton Twin Restoration
Roy Bacon
0 85045 708 4   **£12.95**

Triumph Twin Restoration
Roy Bacon
0 85045 635 5   **£12.95**

GENERAL

British Motorcycles of the 1930s
Roy Bacon
0 85045 657 6   **£14.95**

The Art & Science of Motor Cycle Road Racing 2nd Edition
Peter Clifford
0 905138 35 X   **£12.95**

Ducati Motorcycles
Alan Cathcart
0 85045 510 3   **£11.95**

Honda Gold Wing
Peter Rae
0 85045 567 7   **£6.95**

Motorcycle Chassis Design: the theory and practice
Tony Foale and Vic Willoughby
0 85045 560 X   **£6.95**

Motorcycle Road Racing in the Fifties
Andrew McKinnon
0 85045 405 0   **£8.95**

Superbiking
Blackett Ditchburn
0 85045 487 5   **£4.95**